THE POOR MAN'S WAY TO

RICHES

VOLUME TWO
DAVID BUCKLEY

ISBN 0-933301-38-3

TABLE OF CONTENTS

CONTRIBUTIONS

David Brauner

David Forman

INTRODUCTION

Since writing the first edition of *The Poor Man's Way To Riches,* I've been literally swamped with requests for more money-making information. Many have asked for a "sequel" or a newsletter with more of the same type of information contained in Volume One.

Now, as a result, you are reading Volume Two, which I'm sure you'll find just as rewarding. It seems there is no end to the unbelievable money-making methods available today. Almost every day I receive letters from people telling me how they are making unheard of amounts of cash from their enterprises.

For example, I have direct information on a firm which currently grosses over $60,000 per day! Another somewhat related business has brought its owners upwards of $20,000 per day—from one single product. Both of these businesses can be started on a part-time basis with only a small investment.

Impossible? Try telling these millionaires that! They've ripped the word 'impossible' from their vocabulary. If you're like most of my readers', you will do likewise after reading my books.

To assist you, I will be sending you follow-up letters, from time to time, offering still more volumes in this book. I'm going to do everything in my power to make darn sure you succeed!

In Volume Three I'll tell you all about the $20,000 and $60,000 per day businesses mentioned above—what they are, how you can get in on the same gold mine, and how to do it with only a shoestring investment. I'll also be giving you names of hundreds of companies offering franchises, wholesale merchandise, loans, business opportunities and more.

In the meantime, I hope you find enough methods in this volume to begin making your fortune. Good Luck!

SECTION ONE

HOW TO MAKE $30,000 MONTHLY OPERATING AN OIL LEASE LOTTERY SERVICE

The Federal oil lease lotteries are producing big profits for the government. The government makes a couple of million dollars a month from speculators hoping to win an oil lease from them.

What is an oil lease? Simply put, an oil lease is a legal document giving the holder permission to convey the rights for oil and natural gas found on a given piece of land to a third party.

Thus, if you are lucky enough to win a lease in the monthly drawings (known as simultaneous drawings because all entries received within a one week period are considered as if received simultaneously), you can pay a *"rental fee"* for as long as ten years and receive the right to a portion of the proceeds from any oil or natural gas found on the land.

As a lease holder one may also *"sell"* the rights to a third party, such as an oil company, and keep what are known as the overriding royalty rights to the property. Should you do this, you will receive a flat payment for allowing an oil company to explore for oil on the property, while the override will ensure that you share in the good fortune if oil or natural gas is found.

The leases are available to all American citizens through a simple, inexpensive monthly lottery administered by the Bureau of Land Management (BLM) in the eleven westernmost states. The leases, which range in price from roughly $20 for a 40-acre tract to $1,280 for 2,560 acres (which is the largest possible lease), are available through a drawing held monthly by the BLM. The entry fee is $75. The ultimate return can be more than one million.

It is the chance of a large return that draws in the thousands of entries each month from interested speculators. Actually, most leases are worth considerably less than the one million and quite a few are worth nothing at all. The government only allows citizens to apply for leases on land the BLM believes has no gas or oil under it! If they suspect there is an oil or gas deposit, that land is put in a separate auction by competitive bid.

So it appears the government is running one big con game by taking in millions of dollars from land they are convinced has no value. The only reason people participate in this lottery is because occasionally oil and gas deposits are found on the land and the story receives wide publicity. The reprint from the *National Enquirer* shown later is an example.

Additionally, the price of oil and gas continues to rise and drilling activity is growing in areas previously thought not to contain oil. Therefore, money can be made by selling the rights to oil companies and others who want to drill on the property and oil operators will pay the lease owner a fat profit for drilling rights.

This makes a filing service a big moneymaker for the ones presently in operation—and there is plenty of room for newcomers. People who are now active in the business are making upwards of $30,000 monthly in fees for doing little more than filing the entry cards for their clients. One firm in the southwest is filing a minimum of 4,000 cards a month for clients at ten dollars each. Another charges seven dollars each (that's in addition to the $75 for the BLM). Customers come back month after month, so the repeat business is there.

For the most part, all these services do is offer their clients a list of recommended leases which are sent in advance of the BLM posting. The client then chooses the leases on which he wishes to file and then sends the money to the service.

HOW THE LEASE PROGRAM WORKS

The Bureau of Land Management, a Federal agency, is part of the U.S. Department of Interior, and has 13 offices managing government land in the 50 states. Each office offers its own managed land for lease, so you will have to deal with each office separately when filing for leases.

The lease is for ten years and an annual rental of $1.00 per acre is paid by the lease holder to the BLM. If there is no drilling underway at the end of ten years, or the lessee doesn't pay the annual rental fee, the land reverts to its open status and is put up for simultaneous offering again.

If any lands are available for re-leasing, the BLM State Office posts its list on the first day of business for the months of February, April, June, August, October, and December. Applications are accepted until the close of business on the 15th working day after the list is posted. All applications for simultaneous oil and gas leases must be submitted to the Wyoming State Office:

BLM Land Office, 2515 Warren Ave., PO Box 1818, Cheyenne, WY 82001

The posted list describes leasing units by subdivision, section township, and range. Applicants must use the entry card supplied by BLM offices (Form 3112-6), and may apply for only one lease unit per card. You may not file more than once on the same parcel but any family members or friends over 21 may each file once for the same parcel.

Those not able to travel to BLM offices to obtain copies of the posted lists may have them sent by mail for $5—$10 per list and can also have a list of successful applicants sent for $4 per month. Write the BLM offices for a list of their Copywork Charges. They will send you prices for sending out lists of leases and winners, and also prices on getting information on specific leases offered. This includes any dry holes, survey plots, patents and field notes made by the Bureau (you may make an advance deposit at each office and get copywork material by telephone or mail-order).

If more than one application is received for a given tract, and that is almost always the case, a drawing is held to decide who will get the lease. After the close of the filing period on the 15th working day after the list is posted, a computer-generated random selection is conducted at the Wyoming State Office. One applicant is randomly selected for each numbered parcel. Each applicant is notified of the result of his/her application in the random selection.

HOW TO START AN OIL LEASE LOTTERY SERVICE

There are basically two things you must know to get into this business. First, you must know how to fill out the entry cards for the drawings, and secondly, you must be able to offer guidance to your clients on picking the best leases for filing for.

The Filing Procedure

On the surface, it appears simple enough to file an entry card, but there are several important points that must not be overlooked or an entry card could be disqualified. It is very important that the BLM prefix and parcel number as posted on the list are accurate. Also important is submitting the proper remittance. Ten entries and a check for only $745, and all entries are tossed out. Other reasons which will cause the filing to be disallowed are improperly filled out checks—such as post dated, payee wrong, and of course, late filing. In these cases the BLM will refund the deposits.

The BLM will not refund the deposit if: the entry card is not signed, if there is a duplicate filing on the same parcel, if the social security or tax-payer number is not shown, if the offer is made on the wrong form, or the card is incomplete. If a filing is made in more than one name, all names must appear on the front side and be signed on the back.

In the case of a company filing, it must comply with regulations 43 CFR 3102.4-1. This requires that the names of all interested parties in the filing be given the BLM along with the nature of their interest and a statement of qualifications, plus the signature of each party (all parties must still be American citizens).

A lease winner must pay the rent on the lease ($1.00 per acre for the first year) within 15 of from the receipt of notice such payment is due—not 15 days from the drawing date.

You can't trust the mail, so unless you plan on delivering the cards to the BLM offices in person, you will have to ship entry cards by using an overnight express courier. You will be out of business if you miss just one deadline.

As part of your pitch to clients, play up the difficulty in filing cards promptly and filling them out correctly. This will be one of the benefits of paying for your service. The other benefit is, of course, finding the best leases.

How to Select the Best Leases for Your Clients

The first step is to subscribe to one of the commercial services that evaluates the leases offered. One service is: *Petroleum Investment Company,* 654 South Ninth East, Salt Lake City, UT 84102. They also provide tectonic maps and give custom evaluations of any lease property.

The second thing you can do is contact the BLM office and pay a fee for the information they offer on lease properties, as previously discussed.

You should also acquire a good background knowledge of the oil business. For a free copy of *Geological Survey Circular 725; Geological Estimates of Undiscovered Recoverable Oil and Gas Resources in the United States,* write to: U.S. Geological Survey, National Center, Reston, VA 22092. This will give you a short education in oil terminology and information on U.S. oil reserves.

An excellent book on the subject you should read is *Oil Property Evaluation,* by Richard V. Hughes, $19.95, from Robert E. Krieger Publishing Co., Inc., 645 New York Avenue, Huntington, NY 11725.

Trade publications which you should read regularly are: *Western Oil Reporter,* Box 1917, Denver, CO 80201, and *Oil & Gas Journal,* Box 1260, Tulsa, OK 74101.

How to Advertise Your Service

Advertising your services is almost as simple as advertising in the same manner as your competitors—direct mail and magazine ads. You should write to some of the other firms for their advertising material to see how they make their offer to prospects. Try to make your presentation even better. In the next few pages, a sample sales letter is presented which you may wish to adapt for your own use.

After reading a little sales material from some of the existing filing services, you will probably notice that a certain few of these firms offer to pay the first year's lease payments. This seems to indicate they already have buyers for these leases in advance—and this is another profit you may wish to consider. Many clients would rather take a percentage of a sure thing than gamble on receiving nothing.

REPRINTED FROM NATIONAL ENQUIRER

U.S. Govt. Land Lottery Gives Anyone the Chance to Make a Fortune in Oil Leases

By MAURY M. BREECHER

"We could become millionaires — on an investment of $75! It's fantastic!" Leah Henderson told The EN-QUIRER.

Mrs. Henderson, 40, of Hawthorne, Calif., was talking about the oil and gas lease she won, with her husband, Noel, and friend as partners, in a lottery conducted monthly by the federal Bureau of Land Management (BLM).

"We did it as a lark," bubbled Mrs. Henderson. "We entered the June 1975 lottery, then the July and August lotteries. In August we hit the jackpot!

"We've sold the 10-year rights we won to Union Oil Co. of Midland, Tex., for $78,000 cash and 6¼ percent royalty on any gas or oil the property yields. They haven't started drilling yet, but we're told an average gas well in the area of our lease, Lea County, N. Mex., could bring royalties of $200 a day — and there could be five wells on

LUCKY SPOT: Noel Henderson shows wife Leah the site of lease they sold for $78,000 and 6¼% royalty.

the property!"

Mr. and Mrs. Henderson and their friend, Rachel Conover, paid a $10 fee to BLM to enter each month's lottery. In addition, they used a commercial service which offers advice on which leases to try for. For this service they paid $15, or a total of $25 each lottery.

Said Mrs. Henderson: "We got four offers from oil companies for our lease, did a little bargaining and settled with

Union Oil.

"The first thing I did with their money was run out and buy a new dishwasher and microwave oven. We also bought some new furniture, prepaid our real estate taxes and invested a lot."

Another entrant who hit it big in the oil-and-gas sweepstakes is C.W. Trainer of Austin, Tex., who is in the oil business as an independent.

[Sample of the posted lease notice   Posted 10:00 a.m. August 30, 1975

```
Notice of Lands Available for
     Oil and Gas Filings
                                       ——————— (Parcel No.)
WY-120   W 02640 ◄———————————— (Serial No.)
T 26 N, R 89 W, Carbon◄———————— (Township & Range)
   Sec. 19:  E½                    ——— (County)
   Sec. 20:  SW¼NE¼,W½,SE¼;
   Sec. 27:  S½NW¼,N¼SE¼.          (Legal Description)

            1000.00 A.  (Acreage Offered in Parcel)
```

At this point, you know all you need to know to get started with your own filing service. Do it right and you too have the same potential $30,000 per month business!

(Sample Letter for Your Filing Service)

EVERY MONTH VALUABLE OIL AND GAS LEASES ARE AWARDED TO CITIZENS FOR A SMALL FILING FEE

$50,000—or more—even $100,000 or up to a million from Federal Oil and Gas Leases may sound like an impossible dream to some people.

But to others—it's a fact! They have proven it. Proven that average people just like you and me have the same chance of making a fortune as anyone else—even as much as oil companies do.

With the onset of the gas and oil shortage came a booming business: Gas and Oil exploration! This business, unlike real estate or the stock market, does not require a tremendous outlay of your hard-earned **Cash. YOU CAN PARTICIPATE!**

The U.S. Government says if you are an American citizen over age 21, **YOU CAN PARTICIPATE** in the vast oil and gas land explorations of the Western United States because they are public domain. Overnight, it may **MAKE YOU A MILLIONAIRE...**but only if you file and win, and that's where we can help.

Let me explain how the Federal Land Management of the Federal Government gives every citizen of the United States a chance to participate if they are over the age of 21.

Each month the Bureau of Land Management of the Department of the Interior conducts drawings in the form of a Government Lottery (IT'S LEGAL) whereby both the oil companies and you alike can file for any parcel of land lease offered. Once each month a drawing is held on each parcel of land offered.

Your chance of drawing one of these tracts is the same as Texaco, Gulf Oil Corporation, or any other company since only one application can be filed on any one tract by a company or individual. **IT COULD BE YOU!**

Naturally, the oil companies want the land. To acquire it they must lease it from the person who holds it. And they pay excellent prices of up to $100 and more per acre, plus an overriding royalty. Some of these tracts have a potential value exceeding one million dollars!

Winners can retain or sell their royalty rights. Estimates based on a 3% overriding royalty (royalty payments for production from active wells) could return $1,000 per acre. Overrides have no value, of course, unless a leased parcel is productive. Though most leases never earn royalties, override payments on productive parcels can and have paid royalty payments to winners for years.

There are millions of acres of unexplored Public Lands with good oil and gas potentials. Thousands of acres posted each month include parcels that bring HIGH PRICES.

Examples of some recent parcels offered are:

1,000 acres, Lea County, New Mexico. Township 24S, Range 34E. Profit Potential: Estimated $75,000 to $150,000 cash, plus overriding royalty which could exceed $750,000 in income from oil and/or gas production from active wells.

200 acres, Eddy county, New Mexico. Township 23S, Range 23E. Profit Potential: Estimated $10,000 cash, plus overriding royalty.

1400 acres, Campbell County, Wyoming. Township 43N, Range 74W. Profit potential: Estimated $40,000 to $80,000 cash, plus overriding royalty which could yield over $400,000 in future income for oil and/or gas production from active producing wells.

The Bureau of Land Management (BLM) by law may not otherwise sell, auction, or award the leases except by means of the monthly drawings of applications (Drawing Entry Cards—Form 3112-1) filed by those qualified individuals who are aware of the lease program. Presently, only a fraction of the qualified individuals file applications.

On the THIRD MONDAY of each month, the BLM offices post a new listing on the potential oil and gas producing lands as being available for lease, giving a parcel number and description by lease unit. A period of five working days is permitted for the filing of lease applications with the filing deadline usually being the morning of the FOURTH MONDAY of the same month.

About ten days after the fourth Monday filing deadline, a public drawing is held to determine the winners of the hundreds of leases available that month. The BLM then issues 10-year leases to the winners. If you keep your lease the full ten years, you must pay the government ONE DOLLAR per acre for annual rental. However, if you immediately sell your lease outright, then the new owner from that time is responsible for ALL expenses.

The leases can be terminated at any time by simply not paying the next year's rental when due. The leases are, of course, transferable, and the winners of good leases are usually immediately contacted by oil and gas leasing companies wanting to buy the leases for cash and an overriding royalty interest.

To intelligently participate in this program, it is necessary to have a workable knowledge of the area where the lands are located, knowing the approximate value of the lease and who will be interested in buying it for the highest cash consideration and royalty agreement.

Each month (YOUR COMPANY NAME) evaluates all land offered for lease and selects only those land parcels that have
current activity and are within productive areas. On the basis of our knowledge and experience in oil and gas leasing activities, we are qualified to select leases which can be immediately sold for a profit.

The filing fee ans service fee are tax deductible business expenses. (See IRS Revenue ruling No. 71-191). Lease rental is also deductible.

Always bear in mind this is a lottery pure and simple. There are always more losers than winners, but somebody is going to be awarded these valuable parcels of land. Your chances are not better or worse than the next person's to win these leases.

Shown on the next page is a sample Simultaneous Oil and Gas Entry Card as it should be completed. Fill in your name, address, and social security number on the front side and sign in only one place on the b ack side. DO NOT DATE. We will enter the date and parcel number on your card after we have evaluated and selected the parcel for you at the time of posting.

Drawings are conducted each month by the Bureau of Land Management within one week to ten days after the fourth Monday of that month. If your card is selected, you will be notified by the Department of the Interior and given 15 days to pay the rent of ONE DOLLAR per acre.

The size of the parcels range form 40 to 2,560 acres each. If you are short of funds needed to pay the first year's rent, we can arrange for an interested party to pay the first year's rent providing you assign 50% of the lease over to him.

STAKE YOUR CLAIM TODAY FOR AN OIL LEASE!
Send us an Authorization Form and your Entry Cards right now!

SECTION TWO

LITTLE-KNOWN BUSINESSES THAT CAN MAKE YOU RICH

HOW TO START A RESEARCH SERVICE AND
MAKE A TREMENDOUS FORTUNE

The Nielsen Organization did $238 million in gross business in 1976. Market counselors of Dallas, who specialize in telephone surveys, grossed $7.5 million the same year. Many small research services gross one to five million a year at this game, and it is a business anyone who has access to a library can start.

Literary Research

There are several types of research services and one of the simpler types is to look up information for a client for an hourly search fee. In most literary publications you will find classified advertisements offering research services for writers on a consignment basis, or offers to sell research reports which are prepared in advance.

Political Research

Another type of research is political research. This is truly a large income area in which you can make money during election years and off years. During off years you research the key precincts—showing voter preferences, what the key issues will be in upcoming elections, how events change voting patterns, etc. Almost every candidate will want a copy of this report, and many will hire you for specific jobs once you get going.

During election years, you will be operating a much more active research service throughout the campaigns. At these times, your job will be to keep tabs on the issues primarily by phone surveys, thus keeping up with the latest information.

Marketing Research

The other basic research area is in marketing research. One possible survey you can perform by mail or telephone is a project showing which advertising media (newspaper, radio, TV, direct mail, signs, etc.) the public is most responsive to. This would save the advertiser a lot of money by directing his ad budget where it would do best. Assuming you received $100 from 50 advertisers, then you make $5,000 for that one job.

Perhaps the best way to start either type of research service is to prepare your business stationery and send out a few letters to potential clients to see what the response is, and then take it from there. Once you have commitments from the interested parties, then you do the job. If the research requires a large outlay of capital, such as a national survey, then you can receive financing from a bank by using your client's purchase orders.

Naturally, your research service will stand or fall on your ability to find facts. This is where your library comes into use. To help you I've compiled a listing of books which teach you almost everything you need to know about doing research. Once you understand the system, the rest is fairly easy.

BOOKS WHICH EXPLAIN HOW TO DO RESEARCH

Preparing a Research Paper, A Handbook. Robert M. Schmitz, Reinhart & Co., 1947, 81 pgs.

How & Where to Find the Facts, William Summers, Arco, 219 Park Ave., NY,NY 1003. 400 pgs.

How to Use the Library, Pacific Books, Box 558, Palo Alto, CA $1.

The Scientific Report, How to Prepare It, Williams & Wilkins Co., 428 E. Preston St., Bal., MD

The Technical Report, It's Preparation & Use, Rinehold & Co., NY 492 pgs.

How to Get it From the Government, Stacy V. Jones, NY, E.P. Dutton & Co. 1951. (This explains how to get the Federal Government into your research project and gives special information services, congressional services and more.)

DIRECTORIES

Guide to American Directories for Compiling Mailing Lists, B. Klein & Co., 23, E 22nd St., New York, NY. (This directory is used primarily for compilation of mailing lists.)

National Directories for Use in Marketing, Pamphlet No. 13. Free from the SBA, Washington.

Sources of State Information and State Industrial Directories, Provides a state breakdown of business and industrial lists available through state and local sources. Available from: State Chamber of Commerce Service Dept., Chamber of Commerce of the U.S. 1615 H. St., Washington, DC.

McRae's Blue Book Annual, Gives addresses and trade names of products. 2 vols. McRae's Blue Book Co., 18 E. Huron St., Chicago, IL.

Thomas' Directory of Manufacturers, Lists names of suppliers, producers, and manufacturers in all lines. 4 volume purchasing guide. These are the primary information sources for U.S. made products.

Trade Directories Of The World, Gives information on trade directories for compiling international and commercial sources.

ECONOMIC & MARKETING INFORMATION

U.S. Government Research Reports, Office of Technical Services, U.S. Dept. of Commerce, Washington, D.C. A monthly list of all research reports available to industry.

Monthly Catalog of U.S. Government Publications, Lists all publications printed by the Federal Agencies and congressional organizations. Government Printing Office.

Business Statistics, U.S. Dept. of Commerce, Washington, D.C. Gives figures on basic business indicators since 1929.

County & City Data Book, Bureau of Census, Washington, D.C. Census information on cities and counties.

Industrial Marketing Directory, City by City marketing information.

Rand McNally Commercial Atlas & Marketing Guide, Rand McNally & Co., Box 7600, Chicago, IL. This is a statistical atlas.

Sales Management Survey of Industrial Buying Power, 386 4th Ave., NY, NY. Estimates of local consumer buying power.

United States Government Organizational Manual, Government Printing Office, Washington, DC. List of all agencies and the official organizational handbook of the Federal Government.

MAGAZINE DIRECTORIES

Ayers Directory of Newspaper and Periodicals, NW Ayers & Son, W. Washington Square, Philadelphia, PA. Lists of all publishers in U.S. and Canada and U.S. possessions by geographical area.

Standard Rate & Data, 1740 Ridge Ave., Evanston, IL. Gives advertising rates and circulation of all large circulation trade and specialty publications.

Ulrich's Periodicals Directory, R.R. Bowker Co.,245 West 17th St. New York, NY 10011. Lists over 7500 foreign and domestic periodicals giving basic publishing facts and other data.

British Union-Catalogue of Periodicals, Academic Press, Inc., NY. A record of the periodicals of the world, from the seventeenth century to the present, in British libraries.

Europa, The Encyclopedia of Europe, Lists all principal newspapers and magazines of Europe classified according to subject matter.

Orbis: The Encyclopedia of Non-European Countries, Covers newspapers and periodicals for all the countries outside of Europe.

INDIVIDUALS

Who's Who In America, Marquis-Who's Who, Inc., Marquis Publishing Bldg., Chicago, IL. The most noteworthy people of America in a biographical directory.

Poor's Register of Directors & Executives,—U.S. & Canada. Standard & Poors Corp., 345 Hudson St., New York, NY. Names of major corporation officials by name.

Current Biography, Extensive biographical data on prominent people. Monthly by H.W. Wilson & Co., 950 University Ave., New York, NY.

MAKE $500 WEEKLY BUYING JUNK GOLD

With just a few hours spare time work each week, you can tap into a "goldmine" right in your own community and make upwards of $500 weekly! Almost every home has an assortment of items containing gold lying around—such things as gold rings, medals, watches, cuff links, brooches, earrings, fountain pen points, cigarette lighters, money clips, etc. Since most owners neither know the value of the items, nor where to sell them, they will welcome the opportunity to do business with you. Here are a few terms you should become familiar with in order to begin your business:

Troy Weight: Troy weight is a different measurement than the English measure. 12 ounces equal a pound by Troy weight. 24 grains equal one pennyweight (dwt); 20 pennyweights equal one ounce.

Gold Plated: An electroplating process. Gold plated items are virtually worthless since the amount of gold content is so small. Don't buy gold plated items.

Gold Alloy: Almost all of the gold items you buy will be a gold alloy since few items are 100% pure gold. Usually silver or copper is added to give "hardness." If nickel has been added, then it is called white gold.

Karat: Karat is also represented by the symbol "K." 24 karats is pure gold. 12 karats is 50% gold, etc. A National Stamping Act requires all items containing gold to be stamped with the karat number, but in certain cases you will find items not marked—these you will have to test to determine their gold content.

Gold Filled: A process whereby thin strips of gold are welded onto another metal and rolled under pressure to produce a hard gold surface. Usually it is represented by the mark, "GF."

Rolled Gold: Rolled Gold Plate, or the symbol, "RGP," indicates a similar manufacturing process to gold filled. The difference being that even thinner strips of gold are used. These alloys for RGP and GF items must be 10 karat or more, and 1/20th of the weight must be in gold. On such items they are generally marked "1/20th to 10K."

Ster: Don't mistake the letters, STER for white gold. This is sterling silver.

You will need a troy weight scale and a few pieces of equipment to test the items for gold content. Scientific supply and jewelry supply firms listed in the yellow pages usually sell this type of equipment. Mail-order firms that offer equipment are: *William Dixon, Inc.* 750 Washington Ave., Carlstadt, NJ 07072, and *Keene Engineering*, 9330 Carbin Ave., Northridge, CA 91324.

When you get your equipment, you can test an item for gold content by filing a groove about 1/8 inch deep in the item. Put a drop of nitric acid in this groove. There will be almost no reaction if the item is 18 karat or better. If the acid turns a light shade of brown, then gold is present. If it turns dark brown, there is very little gold content. If the acid turns pink, you have silver in your hands, not gold. Copper or brass is present if the acid turns green. Determining the exact karat content is accomplished with other items you'll receive in your equipment kit.

Each refiner puts out his own quote sheet for the prices they pay for old gold. The prices paid will vary from one firm to another, so it pays to write to several. As for the price you pay for gold you purchase from individuals, that is up to you. Three cents per 'dwt' (pennyweight) is a safe figure. If your customers don't think that's enough, explain that all the items have to be processed, refined, and then re-sold. Make it clear that your offer is all you can afford to pay.

To locate people who have junk gold for sale is as simple as running classified ads in your local paper. You can even make telephone inquiries if you want to. Offer to test and weigh old gold in their home without obligation and you will have plenty of interested people inviting you over—and most people will accept what you tell them their gold is worth.

This is a potential $500+ weekly net income business if you advertise your services enough, and it's a business with little competition. Neither does it require a large overhead, or investment. You can work part-time or full time and make as much money as you want!

The following is a list of firms which purchase scrap gold and scrap silver. Write to several for the best quotes:

Eastman Kodak; 343 State St., Rochester, NY 14650

Englehard Industries; 429 Delancey St., Newark, NJ 07104

Handy and Harman; 850 Third Ave., New York, NY 10022

HOW TO START A SILVER RECLAIMING BUSINESS

Here is method for turning pennies into dollars. In many cases you will be able to obtain waste solutions containing silver at no cost!

Silver is present in photographic film and fixer solution. Photo studios, printers, hospitals, dentists, newspaper and book publishers are some of the sources you can contact about obtaining their waste. Every business which uses photographic film is a potential supplier and will be happy to give you their waste, or sell if for a few pennies.

Recovering the silver is a very simple operation, and one that can bring you a steady income for the rest of your life. As an example, just one gallon of waste fixer solution averages one ounce of recoverable silver—and at the current silver price, this is worth between $6—$7.

There are several methods for recovering this silver and some are better than others. One simple method is to wrap a piece of copper wire or untreated copper mesh around a piece of wood. You then hang this into the solution and leave it there for a couple of days. The copper attracts the silver and you can recover a large portion of it in this manner, but not all of it. Other methods include metallic replacement and chemical precipitation.

To recover silver from used photographic film, you simply dump it in a drum and burn it. Collect the ashes and send them to the refiner.

You can write the Eastman Kodak company for a free booklet which explains how to reclaim silver along with much more technical information. However, if you plan on getting into this business full swing, then you should consider purchasing a commercial recovery machine. Such a machine will allow you to extract more silver in less time. A typical machine will pay for itself in one month's full time operation. Write for more information to: *States Smelting & Refining Company,* 1390 Neubrecht Rd., Lima, OH. 45801 Road, Lima, OH 45808.

START A WATS LINE SERVICE

A WATS line is a wide area telecommunications service. With the advent of WATS line service, a new business has been created—that is, providing a nationwide marketing service for clients. You've probably seen ads which offer a toll-free number for phoning in your order. But, aside from taking orders for products, such a service could profit from other activities as well.

For example, you could solicit magazine or newspaper subscriptions or renewals for a client; you could offer a dealer referral service whereby you referred callers to a manufacturer's local dealer; or you could even coordinate your toll-free WATS line service with a mailing service to send follow-up information to your client's inquiries.

There are several companies already engaged in this type of business, but there is still plenty of room for competition. Start your business by soliciting clients before you rent your line. Try contacting a few advertising agencies and national mail-order advertisers as a test and see how many clients you can come up with.

To get an idea on how the existing firms solicit business, you can call *Answer America* toll-free at; 800-221-2145 and see how they make their presentation, the types of services offered, fees, and so on. If possible, try to "steal" their clients by offering the same service at slightly less cost, or throw in some extra services free.

SELL "SHELL" CORPORATION—MAKE $500+ WEEKLY

This business doesn't require too much explanation. In another section of this book, I've shown you how to form a corporation for under $100. All you need to make money is to "sell" the corporation to an interested party. Many people like the idea of purchasing a ready-made corporation for their business needs to avoid legal fees and long waiting periods for state approval.

You should sell your corporate 'shell' for at least four to five times what it cost you in legal fees. Simply run an ad in your local paper advertising your corporation for sale. Be sure to check with your state concerning their regulations regarding transfer of ownership before you proceed.

MAKE BIG MONEY CLIPPING NEWSPAPERS

Your primary customer for this business is the publisher, large or small, who needs a steady supply of articles for his publication. All publications must have news items for the particular field of interest they serve, and finding this news is not an easy task.

Two of the more important buyers of clippings are trade magazines and newspapers that report developments in a particular business or profession. To start, go to your library and locate the directory of periodicals. Look under the trades listed in the index for a list of publications that serve the fields you plan on servicing.

Next, select just a few of the available categories—you can't be the clipping service for them all, so specialize. Make particular note of the daily or weekly publications because they are your best bet. Write to several of these and send enough money to get a few back issues.

Any publications carrying a large amount of news items are favorable prospects for becoming a client of your clipping service. Compile a list by name and address of the publications that meet this criteria. Alongside their name, list the type of articles they are likely to use.

Once you have developed a file of potential clients (many of whom will normally pay between $2 and $50 per clipping), then you develop your sources of clippings. Start with your local paper, then expand to other local papers in other cities. Determine the type of articles they carry—whether it's heavy on business news, or any of the subjects carried by your potential clients. If it represents a good source of clip material, then get a subscription to it. Better yet, try to get the editor of a local daily to give you the old copies of other local papers when they finish with them. Think up a good reason for your need besides the fact that you're trying to make a buck.

You can also get clippings from other organizations in your area. Good examples are such groups as the Chamber of Commerce, Labor Unions, Fraternal groups, Realty boards, legal newspapers, etc. These sources often contain good clips not found elsewhere.

Remember, you are only looking for local news. National news that comes through the wire services has already been received by your clients.

When you collect your clippings, paste them on separate sheets of your clipping service letterheads. List the name of newspaper, name of town, and the date it appeared. At the bottom, a line should read, "Submitted at Your Regular Rates." Send your clippings and a self-addressed, stamped envelope to the prospective buyer. By using the self-addressed envelope you will either receive a check or your clipping back. Just remember to send the clippings out while they are still NEWS, don't hold them to long a time. Do this and you will make money—not enough to get rich on, of course, but it's an excellent way to increase your income.

HOW TO SELL INFORMATION
ON UNCLAIMED FORTUNES BY MAIL

Here is a business that is related to the missing heir service I discussed in volume one. The difference here is that you make your money by selling reports on estates rather than actually tracking down any heirs for a commission. This variation requires much less effort on your part and can result in as much, or more profit.

Thousands of people would be able to claim their inheritance if they only knew they were heirs, and if they could be found. And sheer greed on the part of most people will enable you to operate a research service which offers people the chance to collect a possible inheritance. Just make absolutely sure that your literature states you are a research service only—not a finder of missing heirs.

You can begin this business with one or more approaches. One would be to locate a single estate (the larger the better), research all the information you can find about the deceased individual, and sell it in report format to all the people listed in the phone book with the last names which are the same.

Another approach is to research the unclaimed estates in every state and make a national mailing which offers the report to potential inheritors. The names and amounts of these estates are generally available in each state's capital. Begin your search there by obtaining a copy of his death certificate.

In each state where an individual has died intestate (without known relatives or beneficiaries), the estate is turned over to a probate official. States have different titles for this official, but it is his job to act as the executor of the deceased's estate. He'll perform a thorough investigation into the bank accounts, real estate holdings, insurance due, and other personal property left behind by the individual.

The probate official is then a good place to look for supplementary information on the estate in question. Such things as the decedent's former places of residence, employment records, bank records, and so on, will usually be included in a probate report. This information, when included in your report will help your customers determine their relationship to the deceased.

You should also make it a point of determining the state laws concerning descent of property from one heir to another and include a copy of each state's law with your report. Along with this, you need to include some basic genealogical information to further assist the individual.

Your sales letter would begin with a headline something like **$987,564.00 is waiting for someone related to John Doe.**

A brief message would explain that an unclaimed estate in the above amount has been uncovered. Then you give a synopsis of the information you've collected—place of employment, former residences, a physical description, and any other data that might enable a relative to recognize him.

Explain that you in no way infer that the recipient of your letter is in fact an heir, but that they may be. Your service is to sell the packaged information to anyone wishing to establish their relationship and file a claim. Include a reply envelope, an order coupon, and then let human greed take it from there.

A couple of books which might assist you in preparing your reports are: *Searching for Your Ancestors* and *Is There a Fortune Waiting for You?*, from Bantam Books, Inc. 414 East Golf Rd., Des Plaines, IL., 60016. (312) 694-4030 The final approach to this operation would be to accumulate several names of persons who have left estates behind, and then give a brief description of the estate in your sales material. This has the added advantage of giving you a much larger audience of potential clients to sell to.

HOW TO START A TELEPHONE SALES AGENCY

There are many ways to make easy money using your telephone. A properly organized operation could even make you wealthy. This is a business you can operate 52 weeks a year and have from one to 100 people working for you.

Here are some of the possible opportunities open to you in phone sales work:

1) Fund raising drives
2) Political campaigning by phone
3) Selling magazine subscriptions
4) Obtaining sales leads for salesmen
5) Become a sales agent for local or national merchadisers
6) Perform surveys and research—marketing, political, etc.
7) Start a business of your own and sell your products by phone

Fund Raising

Many organizations such as Scouting groups, Little Leagues, ecology groups, various churches and charities, are always on the lookout for ways to raise money. Call some of these organizations, explain your phone service and how you can help them sell tickets to such fund raising activities as minicarnivals, stage shows, dances, bingo games, etc.

If they don't plan such activities, then it may be worthwhile to organize them yourself for at least 20 percent of the gross receipts from the event. Either way, your telephone sales agency is a "natural" for promoting these affairs.

For more information on fund raising read: *Techniques of Fundraising,* David Conrad. New York, Lyle Stuart 1974; and *Fund Raising Techniques,* E. Hereward. New York, Beekman, 1969.

Political Campaign Work

With this operation you sell your services to take polls, contact voters, campaign workers, and other work involved in an election year.

Money is in abundance during a political campaign, so work hard on selling your services to the candidates and their parties. Offer to solicit funds by mail, to sell tickets to banquets, dinners, dances, and other campaign functions.

Charge at least $10 per hour for each phone worker you employ—you should have no problem getting this much during an election. Assuming you have 15 workers on 8 hour shifts, then you would gross $1,200 per day!

Selling Magazine Subscriptions

Prospects are everywhere for magazine subscriptions and it is a continuous type of promotion which can result in steady profits. Aside from selling subscriptions, you can also make arrangements with the publishers to sell ad space for them on a commission basis.

To get started, contact magazine subscription brokers such as: *International Circulation Distributors,* 250 West 55th St. New York, NY 10019, or check your yellow pages under **Magazines, subscription agents.** These concerns will provide you with price lists, order blanks, and sales tips.

Also contact your local newspaper to arrange for soliciting subscriptions for them by phone. Try to get the paper to concede some type of special offer as an inducement to new subscribers.

Obtaining Sales Leads

One of the big problems in direct selling is the difficulty in obtaining good sales leads. The salesman doesn't have time, and management doesn't want to. Therefore, there is a great need for an outside phone agency to generate qualified leads.

Perhaps the only way to avoid potential misunderstanding with your clients is to charge a flat hourly rate for this type of phone work. If you try to operate on a "per lead" fee basis, then the quality of your leads will be a continuing subject of debate and an excuse by your client for not paying you. Neither should you operate for a commission of each sale.

BECOME A SALES AGENT FOR MERCHANDISERS

There are two basic areas here in which to operate: One, you can sell specific products for merchants and have orders go through you, whereupon you get a commission from each sale. You won't have too much of a problem convincing merchants to go along with this since they cannot possibly lose a thing. The other area is to simply act as an advertising agency for the firm. You would make calls to announce special sales, grand openings, etc. Obviously, this would have to be organized on a fee basis— preferably whereby you get paid weekly.

One last thought on selling products on a commission basis; make sure your written agreement with the merchant specifies that YOU get paid even if the merchant exhausts his supply of a product. He may not be aware of the tremendous increase in business you could provide him with and might carry only a limited supply of items.

SELL YOUR OWN PRODUCTS BY PHONE

In some cases you may find it profitable to sell your own products by mail on commission and have your telephone sales agency exclusively set up for that purpose. But remember, whether you sell your own product or someone else's, any product sold by phone must be of known quality. Products which are difficult to describe, are of dubious quality, or can be bought elsewhere for the same price should be avoided.

Before selecting a product or signing a contract to sell another product on commission, it would be a good idea to try a "dry run" by phone to see if it will sell. To locate potential products, write to several sources listed elsewhere under the section, *Confidential Directory of High-Discount Merchandise Sources.*

You can also consult the *Thomas Register* at your library. This set of books lists more than 100,000 American manufacturers of various products which you can purchase direct from the factory.

HOW TO SELL BUSINESS SUPPLIES BY MAIL

Selling to businesses is one of the most profitable mail-order operations there is. And while there are many large corporations doing this, there are even more small firms selling their products as well. It is a business you can start with a moderate investment and perhaps become one of those giant corporations yourself.

Since there is a lot of competition in this type of business enterprise, the best angle to use—and one that most smaller businesses are doing—is to specialize.

For example, some business supply houses specialize in selling just writing accessories. In such cases, they don't try to sell just one or two of an item, but go after large lot orders by utilizing premium incentives. Other suppliers specialize in such things as printed stationery, desk accessories, shipping & addressing labels, graphic art supplies, small office machines and so on.

To get into this business, decide on the types of products you wish to specialize in and pick an appropriate company name that describes your field. Operating the business requires the utilization of basic mail order techniques and a careful study of how your competitors operate.

You should also subscribe to trade magazines in the field which give sources of information about new products and equipment being offered. Here is one: *Office Products News*, 645 Stewart Ave., Garden City, NY 11530.

Also check the Thomas Register for other manufacturers.

Here are the names and addresses of other firms in this business. Write to them and ask for a catalog. Check the general appearance of their catalogs, their refund policy, credit policy, and pricing schedule. Your offers will have to be at least as good as theirs to compete.

Write: *The Drawing board, Inc.*, Box 505, Dallas, TX 75221; *Fidelity Products Co.*, 705 Pennsylvania Ave., S., Minneapolis, MN 55246; *Day-Timers*, Box 2368, Allentown, PA 18001; *Regent Standard Forms, Inc.*, Interstate Industrial Park, Bellmawr, NJ 08031; *C & H Distributors, Inc.*, 451-5S. 5th St., Milwaukee, WI 53204; *Baldwin Cooke Co.*, 5714 Dempster St., Morton Grove, IL 60053; *Magnatag Products*, 75 O'Neill Rd., Macedon, NY 14502; *Carl Mfg. Co.*, Lisbon, OH 44432.

EARN UP TO 120% INTEREST ON YOUR SAVINGS EACH YEAR

A *factor* is a person or firm that purchases the accounts receivable of business and professional people. Small business firms which need to increase their cash flow will often times sell their accounts to a factor at a discount. The factor then collects the moneys due over the period of the contract.

Although a factoring business can be as large as you want it to be, the idea is just to operate on a large enough basis, as a private factor, to earn a hefty return on your savings. With the memory of run away inflation still fresh in our minds, there are few investments in which, when inflation rises, you can break even, much less receive a huge return on your investment. The monthly discount on accounts you are going to purchase should be between 2% to 10%—that's a 24% to 120% return on your capital per annum.

Since you will be running the business primarily as an investment, keep the operation simple.

Rule Number One—only handle the 30 and 60 day accounts which have been carefully screened prior to acceptance. Make sure these are long-standing accounts with a consistent history of paying on time. Have your attorney check the credit of your client and the credit of the accounts you propose to factor beforehand.

Rule Number Two—don't factor for retailers handling consumer accounts. Government laws make it difficult to collect on consumer debt. To reduce risk, only factor for firms selling to other firms.

Rule Number Three—check with your attorney before proceeding. This is one area where you can't play lone wolf. Your attorney will have to help you draw up the purchase agreement, detail what recourse you have with accounts that do not pay (set it up where your client has to take these back), find out whether the client should be notified when you have purchased his account, and whether your charges violate usury laws, etc.

It would be a good idea to have your purchase agreement specify that your client will pay all legal fees and court costs on any disputes that may arise. By setting it up right in the beginning, you should stay out of legal trouble and make up to 120% return on your capital.

If you don't have a substantial amount of savings to use, then it's a simple matter to make the bank your partner by offering your receivables as collateral for a bank loan. The interest they charge you will be far less than what you charge your clients. And by handling only 30 day open accounts, you will be able to easily meet your note payments.

HOW TO MAKE MONEY FROM THE OCCULT

Since man's beginning the subject of the occult is one that continues to hold the fascination of many people. Recently, scientific studies into such subjects as telepathy, acupuncture, telekinesis, clairvoyance and the like, have inspired many books and motion pictures which have in turn popularized these arcane subjects.

To sell occult items and make any real profits through retail stores, you'll probably need to be in a large city but most of this stuff can also be sold by mail. Mystical books and courses, charms, potions, and so on, are some of the products that can be profitably sold by mail to a fairly limited audience. The reason for this is the fanaticism of many of the prospects. They are deeply interested in anything that smacks of mind over matter, and for this reason the repeat business is very high.

Some of the areas you may wish to investigate are:

Graphology—predicting a persons future from handwriting analysis

Astrology—something nearly everyone is familiar with and in which computerized services have made several people millionaires

Bio-Rhythms—a once disputed field which many scientists now agree is fact.

Holding seances, reading palms, and fortunetelling in many forms are some things you can do locally or by mail. Always check with the authorities, however, as fortunetelling is prohibited in many areas.

Read some of the tabloids at your supermarket and you'll get an idea of how some entrepreneurs are pushing the occult. You will find full page ads selling such hokum as an Aladdin's Lamp (minus the Genie, of course) which is positively guaranteed to bring you love, riches, and fame or your money back; various pendants, rings, magic spells, lucky charms; miracle water from Lourdes, dirt from the Holy Land, and other such things you wouldn't believe people will buy. Naturally all claims are backed up by the unquestioned testimony of the seller and the "miracles" he achieved—and yet, it is all perfectly legal because nobody can prove that the supernatural does not exist.

Another proven area for profit is starting your own cult. And I certainly do not mean the radical type which promotes mass suicide, dancing naked in a circle, or violating any laws. The big money is in operating a "Mystery School" along the lines of such organizations as the Rosicrucians, the Mayans, Astara, and many others. Most of these schools charge a healthy fee to become a member and receive their "secret" instructions.

To start up a similar organization, you first need to obtain some of their material, and even join their organizations for a time to see exactly what field of instruction satisfies their members. Note their charges, fees, formats, and so on. You should be able to find ads from some of these schools in the magazine, *Fate* (published by Clark Publishing Co., 500 Hyacinth Place, Highland Park, IL 60035.) *Fate* magazine is probably the largest magazine devoted entirely to the occult and if you want to keep abreast of current interests, you should consider subscribing.

Remember when starting your mystery school that there is a tremendous psychological ploy in issuing membership certificates and/or cards to the initiates. The "group involvement" is a powerful motivator behind most people. So play it up by "screening" your member applications, and always make them send you that signed statement saying that they won't reveal any of the sacred knowledge they are blessed to receive.

The leading publishing houses are:

Llewellyn Publications, P.O. Box 3383, PTLA, St. Paul, MN 55101

Wehman Brothers, 156-58 Main St., Hackensack, NJ 07601

Lucis Publishing Co., 866 U.S. Plaza, NY 10017; and *Health Research*, 98 Lafayette St., Mokelumne Hill, CA 95245. Health Research offers around 25,000 different books & courses on occult subjects. The beauty of it is that much of this stuff is so old the copyright expired decades ago and it is now in the public domain—free to copy word for word. The material can also be adapted to create your own books and occult courses.

Wholesale sources for occult items are:
Art Fair, Inc., 80 4th Ave., New York, NY 10003
U.S. Games and Systems, 468 Park Avenue, New York, NY 10016
Haines House of Cards, 2465 Williams Avenue, Cincinnati, OH 45212.

HOW TO COMPILE & SELL NAME LISTS

Compiling and selling name lists is one of the easiest ways I know of to start a **BIG MONEY** business with only a shoestring investment. If you develop a good list that pulls well for your customers, they'll come back time after time with orders of $50, $500, even $1,000 and more at a time!

In the beginning you'll probably want to put your names on gummed 33-up addressing labels (available at stationary stores.) Later you'll need to have your lists fully computerized in zip code sequence for your clients using bulk mail.

Many excellent lists can be compiled from sources in city, county, state, and national records. Some of these are automobile license lists, tax lists, school lists, building permits, lists of government employees, labor reports, incorporation lists, license and permit lists, and vital statistics.

Newspapers are also a fine source for compiling a variety of mailing lists. Among the items in the press that can be used are the following: births and marriage notices, engagement notices, new business, real estate transactions, advertisers, society items, lists of stockholders, etc. There are even markets for death notice name lists.

Perhaps the greatest portion of lists are compiled from national directories. For instance, there is the *Standard Advertising Register* which lists 50,000 + names of sales and advertising personnel; the *National Roster of Realtors Directory* which gives names and addresses of over 65,000 members of Real Estate Boards in the U.S.; *The American Register of Exporters and Importers* which lists over 25,000 importers and exporters; and the *Poor's Register of Directors and Executives* directory giving names and home addresses of over 80,000 business executives.

This doesn't even begin to scratch the surface on the types of directories you can use to compile and sell name lists. You can get lists of coin collectors, doctors, druggists, scientists, ministers, investors, and just about any other kind of list imaginable.

Selling your list after you have compiled it by typing the names on labels is merely a matter of advertising—either classifieds, space ads, or direct mail.

This is a business which takes a little time to get going but it is one which has an almost unlimited potential. The big companies make plenty and they aren't doing anything you can't do as well on a smaller scale.

HOW TO START A SMALL NEWSPAPER

The best way to start a small local newspaper is to plan right off that most of your income will come from advertisers. Some small newspapers are 90% to 100% advertising. How much editorial content you provide is something you can decide for yourself depending on how much time, talent, or other resources you have.

Make no mistake about it—starting a newspaper will probably not break even for at least four months. If you expect this and plan for it, then you will survive and make profits.

The first thing to do is survey the competition. If there is already a paper providing a competitive advertising medium for local businessmen, then perhaps you should look around in another area. Of course, just because an area has newspaper or shopper page coverage doesn't always mean that your paper can't prove competitive. After all, local merchants receive most trade from local people. If the competing paper covers too wide an area, then chances are the businessmen are paying for a lot of advertising distribution in areas unprofitable for them. Point out this fact to local businessmen and they'll easily see the dollars and cents wisdom of dealing with your paper.

One of the strongest sections of your newspaper will be the classified sections and you should work hard to develop this. Check the other papers and call the advertisers by phone if possible. Concentrate heavily on real estate and automotive ad sales since this is where your greatest income will probably derive.

In the beginning distribution will almost have to be free. The least expensive way is simply to place racks at high traffic locations in you town. Later when you expand business, you can hire school boys to deliver papers door-to-door. Some newspapers even offer copies on a "contribution" basis.

Another angle which could help your newspaper through its growing pains is to set up a classified buy-sell-swap page. Consumer advertising is then published at no cost up front. Only when an advertiser sells his product does he pay you the ad cost. There are many publications set up strictly on this basis and they do make a considerable amount of money.

Promote your newspaper. Sometimes the key to something catching on is to use unique promotional methods. Such things as riding a jackass through town with signs advertising your paper, climbing the city flagpole and tossing dollar bills down, having a young lady in a bikini run down main street with you newspaper sign, and other such gimmicks work. These type stunts result in unlimited publicity if you tip off the media beforehand. Be prepared to post bail, however.

Other promotions involve advertiser participation and help get the store traffic flowing. For example, some promotions that have done well in the past are: contests, drawings, lucky license plate promotions, dollar bill serial number prizes, and other things that require a participant to physically step into an advertiser's store.

Some publications that you should subscribe to before beginning are:

Publisher's Weekly, 249 W 17th St., New York, NY.

Publisher's Auxiliary, 491 National Press Bldg., Washington, DC 20045.

Printing Impressions, 401, N. Broad St., Philadelphia, PA 19108.

SECTION THREE

SMART MONEY ANGLES

TO MAKE MONEY FROM OLD STOCK CERTIFICATES

An unusual way to make money is to buy and sell old stock certificates. From time to time newspaper accounts filter through about how someone accidentally discovers old stock previously thought to be worthless. Anyone bright enough to perform a stock search can sometimes realize a considerable fortune through the sale of this stock.

Although the majority of old certificates in existence are indeed worthless, much of it has become valuable through corporate mergers by large existing corporations. Stock from some small insignificant company is absorbed by a corporation like Dupont, General Motors, or perhaps even I.T.T. or some other blue chip firm.

To find out who has these old stock certificates, run an ad in your local paper under the "Wanted" classified heading. Before purchasing large amounts of these old certificates, you can run a "stock search" through a commercial service and discover its value.

FREE PATENTS AVAILABLE FROM NASA & ERDA

Free patents are available from NASA and ERDA (Energy Research & Development Agency), both of which are government agencies head-quartered in Washington, DC. The technology produced through our tax dollars has resulted in literally hundreds of inventions and devices which you can build and market with absolutely no royalty payments.

If you don't wish to become involved in such a manufacturing project, you can still profit by selling information on these free patents to small manufacturers and businessmen who aren't aware of the program. As I've explained in Volume One of PMWTR, government publications are not copyrighted and can be duplicated and sold to others for handsome profit. The ethics of such a practice may be open to question, but it is still 100% legal.

To find out more about these special reports, write to some of the federal agencies listed below:

How NASA Research Development Helps Small Business. A free brochure from the Small Business Administration, Washington, DC.

Patent Licensing Regulations—Reprint of Pages 10446—10448 of the

Federal Register Vol. 27, No. 209. This reprint gives complete information about how NASA handles the public use of the royalty-free patents.

U.S. Patents for NASA Inventions Available. This is a free catalog of some 1,000 NASA patents that are royalty free. These patents deal with such highly sophisticated things as rockets and aircraft, but also lists other items for possible manufacture—such as valves, switches, sound absorbers, spark plugs, and many inventions which might establish you in a small manufacturing business. To receive the catalog and the Patent Licensing Regulations listed above, write to: *Office of General Counsel for Patent Matters,* Code GP, National Aeronautics and Space Administration, Washington, DC 20546.

ERDA, Washington, DC 20545, also has plenty of patents for public use. They have over 4500 patents available to any American citizen—all royalty free. Write them for complete information and catalogs.

ENTER A LOTTERY WHERE YOU CAN'T LOSE

The British Government is operating a lottery which pays out about 90,000 prizes each month—or about $8.75 million altogether. The tickets are called **Premium Savings Bonds.** They are called "Bonds" because they operate like certificates and were created to raise money for the government.

At this writing, tickets cost $2.00 each. If you don't win a prize, your full purchase is refunded! This lottery makes sense when realize that the British Government does NOT pay interest on your savings deposits/tickets. Only a portions of the interest debit is repaid, and that is to the winners of the lottery in the form of prize. The majority of participants receive no prize, and neither do they receive interest.

Every month each bond has a chance to win a prize ranging from $50 up to $10,000. Every three months you have a chance to win a super prize of about $70,000. And as stated, you can redeem you bond at any time and you will receive back exactly what you paid (less any exchange differences).

The biggest problem connected with participating in this lottery is the fact that U.S. laws prohibit communication concerning lotteries through the U.S. mail. There is no restriction against the ownership of British Premium Bonds by United States citizens, but the bonds would have to be held or transferred through a third party out of the country.

One way to participate is to open an account with a reliable bank in Britain and ask the bank to buy the bonds and keep them safe custody—registered in you name of course.

The other way, and the one I prefer, is to use a "mail drop" in Canada, Mexico, or some other foreign country. A mail drop, in case you're not familiar with the term, is simply a firm or individual who (for a fee) will allow you to "rent" his address for a period of time. Thus, only the mail drop in the foreign country would know you actually reside in the United States. Naturally, all mail received by the mail drop would be forwarded to you unopened.

You can purchase these bonds only through a foreign bank or an out-of-the-country mail drop! Any inquiries or correspondence with a United States return address will most likely be ignored. Use your mail drop to write to:

Premium Savings Bond Office, Lytham St. Annes, Lancashire, England

When you buy Premium Savings Bonds, you must wait for three months before your ticket is even thrown in the hat. Once the waiting period is over, you are in for every prize, every month, for as long as you leave your money there. If you hit the jackpot, your prize will be free and clear of British taxes. Winners are notified by mail. Most British papers also publish the number of prize-winning bonds.

If you opt to have a bank handle your lottery affairs, be sure you specify that you want an "external sterling account." Residents of Britain are subject to exchange controls, but these are not imposed on non-residents who hold external accounts.

A few banks you may wish to contact are:

National Westminster Bank Limited, 41 Lothbury, London, England EC2

Midland Bank Limited, 27-32 Poultry, London, England EC2

Lloyds Bank Limited, 71 Lombard St., London, England EC3

Barclay's Bank Limited, 54 Lombard St., London, England EC3

Hambros Limited, 41 Bishopgate, London, England EC2.

HOW TO STEAL A JOB

Method One

Have you ever been to an employment agency to find a job? If so, then you're familiar with the procedure-the agency counselor always calls up an employer, builds you as the best applicant he's ever seen, and sends you on your way to an interview. Chances are that the agency has already sent a dozen other suckers over the same week. Then, when you fail to get the job, you're made to feel as if it were your fault.

Instead of wasting your time and money going through an agency, why not "become" an agency yourself? All you need do is decide what type of job you want, then start calling all the firms in that business and ask to speak to the personnel manager or whoever does the hiring. Once he picks up the phone, you simply go into the same dialogue an employment agency does. In other words, you start explaining that you have a prospect with such and such qualifications, and would like to schedule an interview as soon as possible.

You do not have to represent yourself as an employment agency. Merely the general tone of your conversation and your reference to a "client" is sufficient.

By operating in such a manner you do two things. One, you get through to the person who does the hiring immediately; and two, you use an approach which places you on the same level as the person you're calling. Thus, you can carry on a rather lengthy conversation and discover what jobs are available, what the qualifications are, and if openings are not available, what they will be, and so on.

Method Two

The other method you can use is to go straight to the top. With many firms, a word from a sales manager, production manager, general manager, or other, will result in immediate employment. But, if they can't do it, then go straight to the president if possible.

There are several ways to work this angle. One method is to simply state that you "know" someone in the management end of the business and they sent you. One way to get to "know" someone is to call one of the top executives of the firm and state that you are doing some research—say for a series of articles you're writing—and would like an interview with him to answer some questions, etc. This appeals to his ego and you should have no problems in arranging one.

During the interview, ask "Mr. Big" a few questions to make him appear intelligent and impress him with your go-getter style. Don't mention that you want a job, but make sure he knows you might be interested in a job of that nature in the future. Quiz him about the opportunities, problems, and duties involved with such a position. His ego will naturally swell with pride, and if he doesn't offer you a job right then, it'll be because one isn't available. If no job is offered, try to obtain the names of other people in his position at related firms. You can try these next.

Now, from this interview you go to the personnel manager and leave your resume and application. At anytime in the future when you anticipate an opening, you can call back and state that you discussed the employment position with Mr. Big. If you did any selling job at all, he will remember your most impressive interview, acknowledge to the personnel manager that he spoke with you, and perhaps even recommend you for the position— never suspecting you had planned it that way.

If you work this maneuver in at least 4 to 5 places, I positively guarantee you'll find employment. Of course it may be possible to smooth talk a secretary or receptionist into speaking to Mr. Big for you. You may be able to even bribe her into doing this!

Other Methods

Other methods which are sometimes used are such things as letters of recommendation from former employers, letters of introduction from firms in related businesses (mail drops set-up in company names), letters from large well-known corporations, etc.

Some people will write to major corporations such as IBM, General Motors, and other firms to secure a copy of the corporate letterhead design. Then they type a highly complimentary letter from a fictitious executive and paste the letterhead onto it and have it printed. Armed with half a dozen such letters, one can present an awesome image for an interviewer.

It's also possible to get a complimentary letter from a large corporation by writing the president, or other official and telling him what a fine job he's done. If you lead him to believe you're a large stockholder, your letter stands a good chance of being answered by the president or vice-president himself!

HOW TO BUILD A $20,000 COIN COLLECTION FROM A FEW PENNIES

There is a large and growing market for coins, particularly pennies. Perhaps you have heard about the fantastic profits made in the past from pennies. For example, if you had bought $100 worth of 1943 uncirculated P, D or S pennies, than your investment (as of 1978), would be worth $3,025. Another example: the 1950 uncirculated P-penny roll went from 50-cents (face value) to $15 in only 9 years! If you had invested $10,000 in this coin in 1950, 9 years later you would have amassed $300,000!

Obviously, not all coins will do that well, but some do, and it is not difficult to determine the proper coins for investment. Scarcity is the only thing making a premium market for anything. Scarce here means coins issued between 1909 and 1943. Many of these coins are already scarce in terms of demand and are likely to become more scarce as time goes on.

There are basically three stages of price increase for a coin. One is soon after the coin is issued—many dealers and investors make their money selling **large** quantities of coins. The idea is to sell large quantities of uncirculated 50-cent rolls for $1 or $2. Again, this requires quite a bit of selling and is primarily the domain of the large dealers.

The other price increase occurs after 3 to 5 years—just enough time so the uncirculated rolls have not been available from banks for quite a while. The third stage is when a coin is available at sharp premium prices from investors and dealers—the price being regulated by supply and demand pressures in the market.

There is money to be made in either of the first two stages of coin increases, but initially you should probably begin your program on an investment basis. Operating in the way in which I am about to explain, it will be possible for you to start with a few pennies and pyramid your way to $20,000, or just as easily, $200,000.

You should restrict yourself to collecting coins minted between 1909 and 1943, because there were not many coins minted in that era and there are very few serious collectors. The first step is to study the market and how it operates carefully before you invest one penny. You can start by getting a subscription to *Coin World,* Box 150, Sidney, OH 45365; or any other such coin magazine.

You can get current buy-sell prices from many of the dealers advertising in such magazines. It is important that you buy coins at their buy prices, which is the true value of the coins. This price represents what you can get for the coins now.

To determine the coins to add to your investment program, make a chart listing which coins have the largest difference between their buy and retail price. *Those coins with the largest spread in prices are the ones you want to invest in.* By keeping an accurate chart over a period over a period of months, you can easily determine the market demands for various mint coins.

You can obtain your coins at or near base price by running ads in some of the coin magazines. Many times collectors will be over-stocked with a particular coin and will sell it at slightly above base price. It will also pay to get involved in collecting other types of coins when they are available at special prices. These you can use to trade with dealers who have pennies you need.

Let me emphasize that this is not a get-rich-quick program. It will take many months of study and several years to realize a substantial profit; nevertheless, there are ways to speed up the process.

For example, after you have accumulated quite a few coins, you can become a coin dealer. By building up your stock near base prices, you can re-sell the coins at the full retail price for a greater return. You then can take the profits and begin purchasing other coins indicated on your chart as being on the verge of another base price move. Then you repeat the process. This way you can leverage a few pennies into several thousand dollars!

The final stage of your program will enable you to convert your profits into a $20,000 PLUS bonanza. Once you become a coin dealer and have acquired a few thousand dollars in capital, you proceed to enter the *current year uncirculated coin market*. Assuming you have $2,000 with which to purchase current year uncirculated rolls of coins, you take these coins to a bank to borrow another $2,000 which you then spent on still more uncirculated current year coins! Since, historically the average rate of increase for these coins is roughly 50 percent, at the end of the first year, your investment will be worth $6,000. The interest on the $2,000 should run no more than $200 for a collateralized loan, and even this is tax-deductible along with any cost of advertising and selling coins.

HOW TO MAKE $20,000 WITHIN TWO YEARS

Now, here is how to pyramid your way to $20,000 within one or two years: Each time you borrow $2,000 to purchase more coins at face value, you take the coins to a bank (the same or another), place them down as collateral, borrow ANOTHER $2,000, buy more coins, and continue repeating the process as long as your courage holds out.

The beauty of this system is that you can't lose! After all, you are not investing in risky stocks, bonds or other shaky investments. Your investment is instantly spendable at any time—and your return will average 45 to 50 percent every year! What more could you ask for?

EARN A LIFETIME OF ROYALTIES

Wouldn't it be nice to get rich selling something which costs you nothing? Well, there is a way; it's by selling your ideas to others. No matter if we enter a recession, depression, or whatever, the person who can generate ideas will never remain poor for long.

Your ideas can bring you royalties in two ways. One is to sell the raw ideas to others who in turn market them. Ideas for improving old products, for developing new products, for marketing ideas, and so on, are constantly in demand by businesses.

The other way is to invent things. Invent a better mousetrap, or almost anything which fulfills a need and you can sell the invention.

When submitting ideas to established companies, you will be required to sign a *disclosure waiver* of some type. After all, they may be already working on the very idea you are submitting and don't wish to be sued just because you happened to think up the same idea and submit it.

I've included some forms from firms who pay royalties for ideas they use. They are provided for reference only—always write to a company and ask for their own form before submitting any information.

Warning To Inventors: Never deal with any of the "patent assistance" firms you see advertised. Most of these are thinly disguised rackets which will do little more than take your money. See a good patent attorney instead.

To sum up then, you can make a very good living just by thinking, if you first read all the good books on the subject, write to some of the firms seeking ideas, and stay away from the scams mentioned above.

Some books on the subject that you should read are:

Yate's Guide to Successful Inventing, Selective Books, Clearwater, FL

Turn Your Ideas into Money, by Donald W. Cantin, Hawthorn Books, NY

How to Turn Your Ideas Into a Million Dollars, by Don Kracke, Doubleday & Co., Garden City, NY

Complete Guide to Making Money With Your Ideas & Inventions, by Richard E. Page, Prentice-Hall, Englewood Cliffs, NJ.

HOW TO PROTECT YOUR INVESTMENT FOR TWO YEARS WITHOUT THE EXPENSE OF A PATENT

There are many inventions which have considerable merit but do not warrant the outlay of approximately $1,000 to obtain full 17-year patent protection. *(At least, not before an attempt is made to determine its profit potential.)*

This is the reason for the development of the *Disclosure Document Program*. Under this program, the Patent Office will accept and preserve select patentable concepts for a period of at least two years. Disclosure Documents are any piece of paper disclosing an invention signed by the inventor, the owner or an agent of the owner. It is not a patent application, nor will its receipt date in the Patent Office become the effective filing date of any application for a patent filed in the future; however, this does not lessen the value of the properly submitted document as evidence of the conception of an invention. A Disclosure Document should be a much more credible form of evidence than the self-addressed envelope form often used by inventors.

Although there are no restrictions as to its content, the benefits to be derived from the Disclosure Document will depend directly upon the accuracy of the disclosure's contents. Therefore, you are urged to assure that your document is clear and complete. The explanation of the manner and process of making and using the invention should be in sufficient detail so that a person having ordinary knowledge in the field of the invention would be able to make and use the invention. When the nature of the invention permits, a drawing or sketch should be furnished. The use or utility of the invention should be described, especially in chemical inventions.

A Disclosure Document will be destroyed two years after its receipt date unless a related patent application is filed within those first two years. In a new patent application, the Disclosure Document may be referred to in the letter of transmittal. Disclosure Documents, if accepted, will not be returned. Unless a Disclosure Document needs to be used as evidence, you will not need to refer to it when filing your later patent application; however, if the Disclosure Document is referred to, the document will be preserved by the Patent Office just as in patent applications.

The Disclosure Document must be limited to written matter or drawings on paper or other thin flexible material such as linen or plastic drafting material having dimensions or being folded to a size not exceeding 8½ × 13 inches. Photographs are acceptable. Each page should be numbered and be scribed with a color acceptable and dark enough to be photocopied.

Each Disclosure Document, when submitted, must include a $6 fee, a self-addressed stamped envelope and two copies of a cover letter signed by the inventor stating that he is the inventor and requesting that the enclosed material be received for processing under the Disclosure Document Program. The papers will be stamped by the Patent Office with an identifying number and receipt date and the duplicate request returned to the inventor together with a notice.

For more information you can call the Patents Office in Washington D.C., (703) 557-3378.

SAMPLE REQUEST

Commissioner of Patents
Washington, D.C. 20231

The undersigned, being an inventor of the disclosed invention, requests the enclosed papers be accepted under the Disclosure Document Program and they be preserved for at least two years.

(legal signature) ————————————————————

HOW TO MARKET YOUR PRODUCT FOR AS LITTLE AS $20

Use Package Inserts and Cooperative Mailings

One way to market your product is to use a "package insert" or "cooperative mailing". For example, the Atlantic Richfield Company will send your mailing piece to one thousand of its three million credit card holders. Your literature goes out with other non-competitive offers and with the customer's monthly statements. Bear in mind that these names are top quality and are sent by a company they know and hold in confidence.

There are many other such firms that offer these programs at various prices and in minimum quantities. For more information on cooperative mailing programs, write on your letterhead to: *Dependable List Company,* 120 East 16th St. New York, NY 10003. Also, you can write to some of the firms listed below.

Fredrick of Hollywood
6608 Hollywood Boulevard
Hollywood, CA 90028

Fingerhut Products Company
400 First Ave. North Suite 232
Minneapolis, MN 55401

Walter Drake & Sons, Inc.
Drake Building
Colorado Springs, CO 80940

Selling Through Specialty Salesmen and Agents

Here's how to get 500 people selling your product in as little as 30 days. All you do is recruit salesmen who will handle your product for you. Just place an inexpensive advertisement in one of the salesmen magazines describing the opportunity to make huge profits selling your product. You are now talking the language salesmen love to hear!

Now, don't say that this approach does not work because it does! You will find hundreds of these advertisements in such magazines pitching direct sales opportunities in very glowing terms. In many of these operations, the recruiting firm makes its money not by distributing the product, as you would expect, but from selling kits and samples to salesmen! To get in on this gravy train, simply find a suitable product (many sources for products are listed in the "Directory of Merchandise Sources" section), prepare glowing truthful sales literature stressing the huge profits to be made, then schedule your ads. Pick a good product and you will have a steady income for the next 40 years. Write some of the current advertisers and you will see how such an operation works.

Use P.I. Advertising

Many television and radio stations will accept what is known as per inquiry, or P.I., advertising for commissions. You furnish the sales copy or tape which the announcer reads over the air. Normally, the station will announce their name and address at the end of the commercial so all orders go directly to them. The station keeps maybe 50 percent of the money and sends you the balance along with each customer's name and address for order fulfillment.

This method of advertising is quite common for many radio stations and quite a few television stations. The reason for dealing with you is to fill unsold commercial time.

When approaching a station with your offer, you stand a much better chance of selling them on your P.I. deal if you have a product which sells well on television or radio. Records are a natural, but kitchen gadgets, fad items, and certain other items with wide appeal are often accepted.

To greatly increase you chance of receiving this "riskless" P.I. advertising, you can furnish proof that your product has sold well in other mediums: magazines, direct mail, door-to-door, whatever.

One last thing, there are many firms purporting to sell you a list of radio and television stations which will accept per inquiry advertising. Do not believe it. A station which accepts this advertising one week may not want it the next week. All the lists become obsolete almost as soon as they are printed. Your best bet is to write or phone stations yourself (giving the impression you are an ad agency), or deal with a reputable ad agency.

HOW TO GET FREE ADVERTISING

You can get thousands of dollars worth of **FREE** advertising from any number of publications by sending out well-written news releases. Hundreds of consumer and trade magazines regularly publish free ads and free write-ups of new products which interest the magazine's readers.

The returns from such free ads could result in sales of several hundred or several thousand dollars in orders. One mail order firm received a free ad in Parade which resulted in over 5,000 orders!

Many magazines and newspapers also offer free editorial mentions which can result in hundreds of orders. In some cases, such an editorial mention will pull more orders than a paid advertisement. They are definitely worth going after.

Most all advertising agencies will prepare such a release for you, but you should be able to do just as an effective job yourself. The information on the next page explains what elements are needed to prepare a professional release. All you need is a brief cover letter explaining why readers of the magazine would be interested in hearing about the new product; the news release gives technical information and prices. Finally, you should include a glossy photo of the product.

Assuming you have selected a product and wish to go after free advertising, you simply need to go to your library and secure a copy of Ayers Directory of Newspapers and Periodicals. This massive work lists just about every sizable periodical published in the United States by name, address and circulation. Make a list of EVERY consumer and trade magazine which appears to have the readership likely to be interested in your product. You then simply send your release to every magazine on the list. Granted, only a fraction of the publications will accept your release, you need only a fraction to make a fast bundle.

If you prefer to have someone else handle the release production and mailing you can contact John W. Slawenski, 616 Ninth Street, Union City, NJ 07087. (201) 863-0999.

AN EFFECTIVE RELEASE CONSISTS OF THE FOLLOWING........

A BRIEF BUT POWERFUL LETTER INTRODUCING YOUR PRODUCT TO EACH EDITOR. THIS LETTER WILL ALSO ASK FOR THE WRITE-UP BUT IN A VERY SUBTLE MANNER AND IT'S WRITTEN BY AN EXPERIENCED COPY WRITER WHO HAS AN UNDERSTANDING OF EDITORS AND SPEAKS THEIR LANGUAGE.

THE ACTUAL RELEASE IS WRITTEN BY AN EXPERT TECHNICAL WRITER WHO HAS THE ABILITY TO GIVE THE MOST HUMDRUM PRODUCT A TOUCH OF NEWSWORTHINESS AND EXCITEMENT. THIS IS THE "HEART" OF A RELEASE PACKAGE.

YOUR NAME AND ADDRESS FOR LETTERHEADS, ENVELOPES AND REPLY CARDS (RETURNED BY EDITORS TO INFORM YOU OF FORTHCOMING WRITE-UPS) IS SET IN MODERN TYPE BY SKILLED GRAPHIC ARTIST TO GIVE YOUR RELEASE PACKAGE A PROFESSIONAL "LOOK"

ALSO INCLUDED IS A WHITE NO. 10 BUSINESS ENVELOPE PRINTED WITH YOUR NAME ADDRESS AND "PHOTO DO NOT BEND — FIRST CLASS MAIL". PUBLISHERS NAME ADDRESS WILL BE TYPED ON THESE ENVELOPES.

YOUR GLOSSY PHOTOGRAPH WILL BE REPRODUCED BY MODERN PHOTOGRAPHIC EQUIPMENT. IF NECESSARY, OUR EXPERIENCED CAMERA MEN WILL PHOTOGRAPH YOUR PRODUCT AT A SMALL ADDITIONAL CHARGE. A GOOD DESCRIPTIVE PHOTO IS A "MUST" FOR YOUR RELEASE TO BE EFFECTIVE

LETTERS, RELEASES, REPLY CARDS, ENVELOPES ARE THEN PRINTED, FOLDED, COLLATED, PACKAGED AND SHIPPED TO YOU BY OUR FAST, EFFICIENT PRODUCTION DEPARTMENT. WE DO JUST ABOUT EVERYTHING.... ALL YOU HAVE TO DO IS APPLY POSTAGE AND DROP IN MAIL BOX OR POST OFFICE.

AN INVENTION NEWS RELEASE CONSISTS OF THE FOLLOWING:

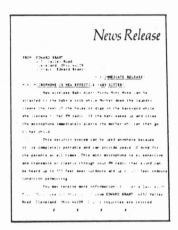

A news release which describes your invention fully and clearly.

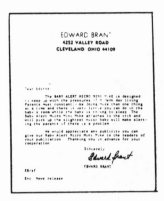

A hard hitting letter to the editor asking to have your new invention featured. This letter will have your name and address professionally printed on top.

A No. 10 business envelope printed professionally with your name and address on left and addressed to the best suited publications for your particular invention.

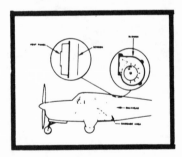

A picture of your patent drawing or of your actual invention which editors will use in their write up of your invention.

You send these Invention News Releases to the publications which relate to it, and then the editors will hopefully select your invention for FREE publicity in their magazines. The ad will likely be seen then by the "key" people who can produce and market your invention.

Mailing out Invention News Releases is one of the most effective ways to reach the right people in your industry that can do you the most good.

You send these Invention News Releases to the publications which relate to it, and then the editors will hopefully select you invention for FREE publicity in their magazines. The ad will likely be seen then by the key people who can produce and market your invention.

Mailing out Invention News Releases is one of the most effective ways to reach the right people in the industry who can do you the most good.

SECTION FOUR

EARN LARGE FEES AS A "FINDER" OF EXECUTIVES

In volume one of, *"The Poor Man's Way to Riches,"* I explained how to get started as a finder of goods, services, or situations for someone else. Another area you should consider is finding executives who are much in demand by large corporations.

Check the business and classified sections of your local newspaper on any given day and you'll find ads offering employment to a very large number of qualified executives or other special personnel. Call or write the firms advertising and ask if they offer a finder's fee for locating the executive.

Be sure you have some professional looking letterheads printed up when you write, and have your client sign a copy of the enclosed FINDER AGREEMENT before you reveal the name of the executive.

Once you have a number of assignments, you then run ads describing these positions in business journals, magazines, and newspapers where your clients aren't advertising. Another way to get started is to become a subcontractor for *Executive Search Firms* (employment agencies).

Naturally, not all search firms will accept subcontractors but many will. And while your fees may be slightly less, it's an excellent way to begin. On the next few pages are addresses of firms who may be willing to use subcontractors. Search through your local newspaper for more sources.

Hallmark Personnel Consultants, Inc.
5851 E. Speedway
Tuscon, AZ 85712
602-885-2345

Henry Labus Personnel
820 Ford Bldg.
Detroit, MI 48201
313-962-4461

Dunhill Personnel System
One Old Country Rd.
Carle Place, NY 11514

Sales Consultants
1127 Euclid Ave., #1400
Cleveland, OH 44115-1638

Baker and Baker Employment Service
PO Box 364
Athens, TN 37303

Hayes Personnel Service
25 N. Cascade #208
Colorado Springs, CO 80903

Atlantic Personnel Services
4806 Shelly Dr.
Wilmington, NC 28405

Ameribiz Employment
167 S. River Rd.
Bedford, NH 03102

Management Recruiters
1127 Euclid Ave. #1400
Cleveland, OH 44115-1638

Sanford Rose Associates
265 S. Main St.
Akron, OH 44308

F-O-R-T-U-N-E Personnel Consultants
655 Third Ave. #1805
New York, NY 10017

Bailey Employment Service
51 Shelton Rd.
Monroe, CT 06468

Career Exchange Center
6992 El Camino #104-439
Carlsbad, CA 92008

Best Resume Service/Best Executive Mktg.
625 Stanwix St.
Pittsburgh, PA 15222

Business & Professional Consultants
3255 Wilshire Blvd. #1732
Los Angeles, CA 90010

AGREEMENT TO PAY FINDER'S FEE

_____, hereafter termed the FINDER, and _____
_____, hereafter termed the CLIENT, hereby declare and agree,
on this _____ day of _____, that the FINDER will be paid fee
of _____ to find for the Client the following
_____. This fee will be paid to the FINDER by the CLIENT
within 10 days after the FINDER has delivered to the CLIENT, or arranged for the
delivery to the CLIENT, the above-mentioned article.

As evidence of their consent to this agreement, both the CLIENT and FINDER have
signed this agreement as shown below.

_____   _____

FINDER-Date   CLIENT-Date

_____   _____

WITNESS   WITNESS

SECTION FIVE

HOW TO OBTAIN GRANTS & LOANS FROM FOUNDATIONS

WHAT ARE FOUNDATIONS?

Foundations are non-profit corporations set up to benefit mankind in some way. They are usually organized by wealthy individuals, corporations and other organizations that distribute the funds for specific purposes.

In a recent year, 10,426 grants were made throughout 43 states and totaled $784 million! The purpose for which this money was distributed ranged from education and welfare to the sciences; from health and humanities to religion. Most grants went to non-profit organizations performing humanitarian work, but it is not unusual for foundations to aid individuals through organizations they support.

Some foundations have special funds for emergency grants to individuals. Any attorney who has done work before with foundations can help you in this regard.

HOW TO PREPARE A PROPOSAL

A paper produced by the staff of The Foundation Center of the University of California recommends a two-step approach. Initial inquiry should be made by letter or in person to a specific foundation, or a form letter to many foundations with a summary of the proposal which stresses how the grant will further the purpose of the foundation.

If the foundation's directors feel you may be eligible for a grant, they may request a more complete application. Be prepared to supply the following information:

1. A summary of the organization applying for a grant—its purpose, accomplishments, names and qualifications of the directors and staff.

2. Specific details on the program proposed—what the aim is, whether national or international operations are involved, etc. Include endorsements and certifications by prominent citizens or authorities on the project feasibility.

3. Financing strategy—List where primary financial assistance will come from . . . government, individuals, the foundation, or other organizations.

4. Keep initial requests under $10,000 until you have established a working project. In This way a request for amounts exceeding $100,000 becomes a definite possibility.

5. Furnish proof that no other private or public institutions are already providing the services or programs you will be doing.

6. List the names of qualified professionals who will be consulted on the project—attorneys, accountants, bankers, etc.

7. Submit copies of your last annual report or audit. If none are issued, furnish a statement on income, expenditures and programs for the past year.

One service available to grant seekers is the Foundation Grants Data Bank which is a compilation of 14,000 grants. For more information, contact the Foundation Center, 79 5th Ave., New York, NY 10019

The Ahmanson Foundation
3731 Wilshire Blvd.
Los Angeles, CA 90010
(213) 383-1381

Alcoa Foundation
1501 Alcoa Building
Pittsburgh, PA 15219
(412) 553-4696

DeRance, Inc.
7700 West Blue Mound Rd.
Milwaukee, WI 53213
(414) 475-7700

Disney Foundation
c/o Shamrock Holding Inc.
PO Box 7774
4421 Riverside Dr. Suite 207
Burbank, CA 91510

The Kresgoe Foundation
PO Box 3251 W. Big Beaver Rd.
Troy, MI 48007-3151
(313) 643-9630

Lilly Endowment, Inc.
2801 North Meridian St.
Indianapolis, IN 46208

Vincent Astor Foundation
405 Park Ave.
New York, NY 10022

Atlantic Richfield Foundation
515 South Flower St.
Los Angeles, CA 90071
(213) 486-3342

Carnegie Foundation of New York
437 Madison Ave.
New York, NY
(212) 371-3200

The Cleveland Foundation
1400 Hanna Bldg.
Cleveland, OH 44115

The Commonwealth Foundation
One East 75th. St.
New York, NY 10021
(212) 535-0400

The Cullen Foundation
PO Box 1600
Houston, TX 77251

Edna McMonnell Clark
Foundation
250 Park Ave.
New York, NY 10017
(212) 986-7050

Danforth Foundation
222 South Central Ave. St.
Louis, MO 63105

The San Francisco Foundation
500 Washington St. 8th floor
San Francisco, CA 94111
(415) 392-0600

The Ford Foundation
320 East 43rd. St.
New York, NY 10017
(212) 573-5000

F.E. Gannett Newspaper Found.
One Lincoln Tower
Rochester, NY 14604
(716) 262-3315

Gulf Oil Foundation
439 7th Ave.
Pittsburgh, PA 15230
(412) 263-5968

Houston Endowment
PO Box 52338
Houston, TX 77052
(713) 223-4043

The James Irvine Foundation
One Market Plaza
San Francisco, CA 94105
(415) 777-2244

W.K. Kellogg Foundation
400 North Ave.
Battle Creek, MI 49017-3398
(616) 968-1611

William R. Kenan, Jr. Trust
120 Broadway
New York, NY 10271
(212) 732-3151

Turrell Fund
33 Evergreen
East Orange, NJ 07018

Andrews M. Mellon Foundation
140 East 62nd. St.
Pittsburgh, PA 15219
(212) 838-8400

Charles Stewart Mott Foundation
500 Mott Fondation
Flint, MI 48502

Richard King Mellon Foundation
525 William Penn Place
Pittsburg, PA 15219
(412) 392-2800

New York Community Trust
415 Madison Ave.
New York , NY 10017
(212) 758-0100

William Penn Foundation
1630 Locust St.
Philadelphia, PA 19103
(215) 732-5114

The Pew Memorial Trust
229 S. 18th St.
Philadelphia, PA 19102
(215) 875-3200

The Rockefeller Foundation
1133 Avenue of the Americas
New York, NY 10036
(212) 869-8500

Rockefeller Brothers Fund
1290 Ave. Of Americas
New York, NY 10104

Ford Motor Company Fund
The American Rd.
Dearborn, MI 48121
(313) 845-8711

Sarah Scaife Foundation, Inc.
PO Box 268
Pittsburgh, PA 15230

Alfred P. Sloan Foundation
630 5th Ave.
New York, NY 10111
(212) 582-0450

The Surdna Foundation
260 Park Ave.
New York, NY 10177
(212) 697-0630

United States Steel Foundation
600 Grant
Pittsburgh, PA 15230

Robert A. Welch Foundation
4605 Post Oak Pl.
Houston, TX 77027

Green Island Inc.
c/o Grabill and Ley, Inc.
Ten Post Office Sq.
Boston, MA 02109

Grass Foundation
77 Reservoir
Quincy, MA 02170
(617) 773-0002

George Harrington Trust
c/o Boston Safe Deposit &
Trust Company
One Boston Pl.
Boston, MS 02106
(617) 722-7318

Blanchard Foundation
c/o Boston Safe
One Boston Pl.
Boston, MS 02106

Old Colony Charitable Foundation
c/o First National Bank Of Boston
PO Box 1890
Boston, MS 02105
(617) 434-5669

Perpetual Benevolent Fund
c/o Bay Bank Middlesex:
300 Washington St.
Newton, MS 02158

Adams Memorial Fund
c/o The First National Of Boston
PO Box 1890
Boston, MS 02105

Warren Benevolent Fund
342 Eliot St.
PO Box 46
Ashland, MS 01721
(617) 434-5669

Fidelity Foundation
82 Devonshire St.
Boston, MS 02109

Phillips Foundation
13 College Hwy.
Lyme, MS 03768
(603) 795-2790

Xerox Foundation
PO Box 1600
Stamford, MS 06904
(203) 329-8700

Kayser-Roth Foundation
c/o Gulf & Western Industries, Inc.
High Ridge Park
Stamford, CT 06904

Bissell Foundation
One Constitutional Plaza 12th fl.
Hartford, CT 06103
(203) 521-6528

Banburry Fund, Inc.
101 Park Ave 35th fl.
New York, NY 10178

Kidder Peabody Foundation
20 Exchange Pl.
New York, NY 10005

Ederic Foundation, Inc.
A-102 Greenville Center
3801 Kennett Pike
Wilmington, DL 19807

Fairchild Industries
20301 Century Blvd.
Germantown, MD 20874

Baldwin Foundation
Two Hopkins Plaza
Baltimore, MD 21201

James W. Colgan Trust
1391 Main St.
PO Box 9003
Springfield, IL 01101
(413) 787-8700

Boston Foundation
One Boston Place
Boston, MS 02108
(617) 723-7415

Cabot Foundation, Inc.
125 High St.
Boston, MA 02110
(617) 423-6000

Ellison Foundation
129 South St.
Boston, MA 02111

Charles Hood Dairy Foundation
500 Rutherford Ave.
Boston, MA 02111

Cambridge Foundation
99 Bishop Allen Dr.
Cambridge, MA 02139
(617) 876-5214

Henderson Foundation
PO Box 420
Sudbury, MA 01176
(617) 443-4646

Pilgrim Foundation
8 Perkins Ave.
Brockton, MA 02401
(617) 586-6100

Textron Foundation Trust
PO Box 878
Providence, RI 02901
(401) 421-2800

Barker Foundation
PO Box 328
Nashua, NH 03301

Olin Scott Fund, Inc.
100 South St.
PO Box 1208
Bennington, VT 05201

Heublein Foundation
PO Box 388
Farmington, CT 06032
(203) 677-4061

Fox Foundation
c/o Connecticut Nat. Bank
777 Main St.
Hartford, CT 06115

Morris Joseloff Foundation
125 La Salee Rd.
West Hartford, CT 06107

Maguire Foundation
One Atlantic St.
Stanford, CT 06904

Annie E. Casey Foundation
51 Weaver St.
Greenwich, CT 06830

Alix W. Stanley Foundation
PO Box 1318
New Britain, CT 06050
(303) 224-6473

David Schwartz Foundation
50 Terminal Rd.
Seacaucus, NJ 07094
(201) 867-9350

Fannie E. Rippel Foundation
333 Main St.
Madison, NJ 07940

Lautenberg Foundation
PO Box 9
Roseland, NJ 07068

Warner-Lambert Charitable FDN
201 Tabor Rd.
Morris, NJ 07950
(201) 540-2243

The Clark Foundation
30 Wall St.
New York, NY 10005
(212) 285-5000

Ametek Foundation
410 Park Ave.
New York, NY 10022
(212) 935-8640

Dow Jones Foundation
22 Cortland St.
New York, NY 10007
(212) 285-5000

Dun & Bradstreet Co's FDN
299 Park Avenue
New York, NY 10171

Allied Stores Foundation, Inc.
1114 Ave. Americas
New York, NY 10036
(212) 764-2333

Mobile Foundation Inc.
150 East 42nd. St.
New York, NY 10017
(212) 883-2174

The Ford Foundation
320 E. 43rd St.
New York, NY 10017

Bydale Foundation
500 5th Ave.
New York, NY 10110

Biddle Foundation, Inc.
61 Broadway Rm. 2912
New York, NY 10006

The Grossman Foundation
1440 Broadway
New York, NY 10018

Gilman Foundation, Inc.
111 W. 50th St.
New York, NY 10020
(212) 246-3300

Avon Products Foundation
713 Park Ave.
New York, NY 10022

The Mailman Foundation
460 Park Ave.
New York, NY 10022

Bendheim Foundation
Ten Columbia Cr.
New York, NY 10019

List Foundation
Byram Shore Rd.
Byram, CT 10573

Knox Family Foundation
PO Box 387
Johnstown, NY 12095

J.M. McDonald Foundation, Inc.
2057 East River Rd.
Cortland, NY 13045

Allyn Foundation, Inc.
PO Box 22
Skaneateles, NY 13152
(315) 252-7618

Alcoa Foundation
1501 Alcoa Building
Pittsburg, PA 15219

Horace B. Packer Foundation
61 Main St.
Wellsboro, PA 16901

The Hershey Foods Corp Fund
14 E. Chocolate Ave.
Hershey, PA 17033
(717) 534-7574

Scholler Foundation
2000 Two Penn Center Plaza
Philadelphia, PA 19102
(215) 568-7500

Lovett Foundation Inc.
82 Governor Printz Blvd.
Claymont, DE 19703
(302) 798-6604

John B. Lynch Scholarship FND
PO Box 4248
Wilmington, DE 19807-0248

Copeland Andelot Foundation
2100 Depont Building
Wilmington, DE 19898

Roskob Foundation, Inc.
PO Box 4019
Wilmington, DE 19807

Beneficial Foundation
1100 Carr Rd. Box 911
Wilmington, DE 19899
(302) 798-0800

Merkle Foundation
732 Mansey Bldg.
Washington, DC 20004

Alvord Foundation
918 16th St. N.W.
Washington D.C. 20005

Middendorf Foundation, Inc.
803 Cathedral
Baltimore, MD 21202

Woodside Mills Foundation
PO Box 6126 Sta. B
Greenville, SC 29606

Albert Steiner Charitable Fund
3451 Paces Ferry Rd.
Atlanta, GA 30327
(404) 237-8736

Joseph Whitehead Foundation
1400 Peachtree St., N.W.
Atlanta, GA 30303

Wehadke Foundation, Inc.
PO Box 150
West Point, GA 31833

Simon Schwab Foundation
PO Box 1014
Columbus, GA 31902

Pickett & Hatcher EDC Fund
PO Box 8169
Columbus, GA 31908
(404) 327-6586

Malbis Memorial Foundation
PO Box 218
Daphen, AL 36526

Mitchel Foundation
PO Box 1126
Mobile, AL 36606

Bernal Foundation
1400 8th Ave. North
Nashville, TN 37202

Margolin Foundation
1028 North Hollywood
Memphis, TN 38108

Deposit Guaranty Foundation
PO Box 1200
Jackson, MS 39201

Elizabeth Irby Foundation
PO Box 1819
Jackson, MS 39205

Hazard Memorial Foundation
515 S. 2nd. Ave.
Columbus, MS 39701

Shapira Foundation
528 W. Main St.
Louisville, KY 40202

Haskin Foundation
200 E. Broadway
Louisville, KY 40204

Bremer Foundation
708-9 Union Nat. Bank Bldg.
Youngstown, OH 44503

Firestone Foundation
1200 Firestone Pkwy
Akron, OH 44317
(216) 379-6802

The Dayton Foundation
1395 Kattering Tower
Dayton, OH 45423

Liberty Fund, Inc.
7440 N Shadeland
Indianapolis, IN 46285
(317) 842-0880

Lilly Endowment, Inc.
Lilly Corporate Center
Indianapolis, IN 46285

Miles Laboratories Foundation
1127 Myrtle St.
Elkhart, IN 46515
(219) 423-6419

Smock Foundation
116 E. Berry St.
Fort Wayne, IN 46802
(219) 423-6419

Thrush Foundation, Inc.
PO Box 185
Peru, IN 46970

Earhart Foundation
Plymouth Bldg. St. 204
Ann Arbor, MI 48105

Henry Ford II Fund
100 Renaissance Center
Detroit, MI 48243

Herrick Foundation
2500 Comerica Bldg.
Detroit, MI 48226

Whiting Foundation
PO Box 1980
Sun Valley, ID 83353

Bohen Foundation
1716 Locust St.
Des Moines, IA 50336

Joh Ruan Foundation Trust
3200 Ruan Center
Des Moines, IA 50304

Gardner Cowless Foundation
Register & Tribune Bldg.
Des Moines, IA 50304

Younkers Charitable Trust
PO Box 957
Des Moines, IA 50304

Ellis I. Levitt Welfare Fund
312 Hubbell Bldg.
Des Moins, IA 50309

Frederic C. Wehr Foundation, Inc.
2100 Marine Plaza
Milwaukee, WI 53202

Tozer Foundation, Inc.
104 N. Main St.
Stillwater, MN 55082

Grain Terminal Foundation
1667 Snelling Ave. North
St. Paul, MN 55164

Phillips Foundation
100 Washington Sq.
Minneapolis, MN 55401
(612) 331-6230

Minneapolis Foundation
821 Marquette Ave.
Minneapolis, MN 55402

The Hubbard Foundation
3415 University Ave., S.E.
Minneapolis, MN 55414

General Mills Foundation
9200 Wayzata Blvd.
Minneapolis, MN 55440

Walgreen Benefit Fund
200 Wilmot Rd.
Deerfield, IL 60015

Allstate Foundation
Allstate Plaza, F-3
Northbrook, IL 60062

Retirement Research Foundation
325 Touhy Ave.
Park Ridge, IL 60068

Brunswick Foundation
One Brunswick Plaza
Skokie, IL 60077

Keating Family Foundation
640 Winnetka Mews
Winnetka, IL 60093

Andrew Foundation
10555 W. 153rd. St.
Orland Park, IL 60462

Stone Foundation
360 N. Michigan Ave.
Chicago, IL 60601

Bowyer Foundation
135 S. La Salle St., Ste. 1500
Chicago, IL 60603

Rice Foundation
222 Waukigan Rd.
Glenview, IL 60025

Marquette Charitable Organ.
2141 S. Jefferson St.
Chicago, IL 60610

Stewart-Warner Foundation
1826 Deversey Parkway
Chicago, IL 60614

Cuneo Foundation
2 N. Riverside Plaza
Chicago, IL 60606

Walter E. Heller Foundation
3400 Xerox Center
Chicago, IL 60603

Robert Galvin Foundation
1303 E. Algoneuin Rd.
Chicago, IL 60646

Oscar Mayer Foundation, Inc.
115 S. La Salle St.
Chicago, IL 60603

Crane Fund for Widows and Children
222 West Adams St.
Chicago, IL 60606

Bersted Foundation
30 N. La Salle
Chicago, IL 60697

Smith Charitable Trust
850 Church St.
Rockford, IL 61103

John Deere Foundation
John Deere Rd.
Moline, IL 61262

May Store Foundation
601 Olive St.
St. Louis, MO 63101

Westwood Charitable FND
10712 Kahlmeyer Dr.
St. Louis, MO 63132

Monsanto Fund
800 N. Lindbergh Blvd.
St. Louis, MO 63167

Pillsbury Foundation
Six Oakleigh Ln.
St. Louis, MO 63124

Smith Foundation
PO Box 38
Kansas City, MO 64183

Kemper Charitable Trust
10th and Grand Ave.
Kansas City, MO 64141

Whitaker Foundation
7711 Bohomme Ave.
St. Louis, MO 63105

The Commerce Foundation
P.O. Box 13686
Kansas City, MO 64199

David W. Kemper Mem. FND
PO Box 135861
Kansas City, MO 64199

Townsend Educational Fund
PO Box 147 St.
Joseph, MO 64502

Jellison Benevolent Society
PO Box 88
Topeka, KS 66601

Jones Foundation
515 Citizen's NTL. Bank Bldg.
Emporia, KS 66801

Swanson Foundation
8401 W. Dodge St.
Omaha, NE 68114

Steinhart Foundation Inc.
1000 Terrace Dr.
Nebraska City, NE 68401

George T. Able Memorial FDN
PO Box 80268
Lincoln, NE 68501

Mc Donald Foundation, Inc.
PO Box 202
Hastings, NE 68901

Freeman Foundation
PO Box 50400
New Orleans, LA 70150

Zemurray Foundation
335 Whitney Bank Blvd.
New Orleans, LA 70130

Bass Foundation
4224 Thanksgiving
Tower Dallas, TX 75d201

Florence Foundation
PO Box 241
Dallas, TX 75221

Hillcrest Foundation
PO Box 83791
Dallas, TX 75283

Shell Companies Foundation, Inc.
Two Shell Plaza
PO Box 2009
Houston, TX 77002

Worthan Foundation
2777 Allen Parkway
Houston, TX 77019

Silver Foundation
1506 National Bank Bldg.
Denver, CO 80293

A.V. Hunter Trust, Inc.
633 17th St., STE 1600
Denver, CO 80202

Hill Foundation
707 17th St.
Denver, CO 80202

Gates Foundation
150 S. Madison
Denver, CO 80209

Jack Petteys Memorial Fund
PO Box 324
Brush, CO 80723

Thatcher Foundation
PO Box 1401
Pueblo, CO 81002

Marshal Foundation
PO Box 3306
Tucson, AZ 85722

The Phillips Foundation
PO Box 1098
Palm Desert, CA 92260

Frank R. Seaver Trust
900 Wilshire Blvd.
Los Angeles, CA 90017

Battistone Foundation
PO Box 3858
Santa Barbara, CA 90052

Whitier Foundation
1600 Huntington Dr. South
Pasadena, CA 91030

Earl B. Gilmore Foundation
6301 W. 3rd
Los Angeles, CA 90036

Elbridge Stuart Foundation
PO Box Terminal Annex
Los Angeles, CA 90051

The Samuel Goldwyn Foundation
10203 Santa Monica Blvd.
Los Angles, CA 90067

Conrad N. Hilton Foundation
10101 Santa Monica Blvd. #775
Los Angeles, CA 90067

Ralph B. Lloyd Foundation
9441 Olympic Blvd.
Beverly Hills, CA 90212

The Shea Foundation
655 Brea Canyon Rd.
Walnut, CA 91789

Simon Foundation
411 W Colorado Blvd.
Pasadena, CA 91105

Trust Funds, Inc.
100 Broadway
San Francisco, CA 94111

Swig Foundation
Fairmont Hotel
San Francisco, CA 94106

Hawaiian Foundation
PO Box 3170
Honolulu, HI 96802

SECTION SIX

SPECIAL LOAN SOURCES

SEVEN OFF SHORE BIG MONEY LENDERS

Amsterdam Rottendam Bank
PO Box 1220
Amsterdam 1000, Holland

Pinansbanken
PO Box 298
DK K501 Copenhagen v. Denmark

Swiss Bank Corporation
Aesschenvorstadt I
4022 Basel, Switzerland

Swiss Credit Bank
Paradelatz
8022 Zurich, Switzerland

Bank of Oman Limited
Head Office
Dubai United Arab Emirates
PO Box 1250
6-8 Nue de la Rotisserie
1204 Geneva Switzerland

de Berig S.A.
13 Ave Hrieg
1208 Geneva/Switzerland

For a more complete list, check under the 'EUROPEAN BANKING' heading in your local library.

SPECIAL LOAN SOURCE FOR RURAL FAMILY LOANS
Farm Credit Administration
490 L'Enfant Plaza West
Washington, D.C. 20578

SPECIAL LOAN SOURCE FOR CURRENT & FORMER GOVERNMENT & MILITARY EMPLOYEES

Government Employee's
Financial Corp.
7551 West Alameda Ave.
Lakewood, CO 80226

FINANCIAL CONSULTANTS

All State Capital Corporation
405 Montgomery
San Francisco, CA 94104

Consolidated Acceptance Corp.
10047 S. Western
Chicago, IL 60643

L.J. Gombar
12591 Glenfield
Detroit, MI 48213

United Security Corp.
36 Kennedy Plaza
Providence, RI 02903

Credit-Care, Inc.
ATTN: Miss Paul Dept: P-725
PO Box 1052
Birmingham, AL 35201

Allied Acceptance
3003 W. Northern Ave.
Suite 1 Dept. NCC
Phoenix, AZ 85021
(602) 995-9777

Town and Country Acceptance
PO Box 26396
Dept. 3394
Birmingham, AL 35226
(205) 823-4930

Financial Services
PO Box 174 DEPT: 774
Fishkill, NY 12524
(914) 896-5015

Suburban Finance Company
PO Box 144
Jamaica, NY 11415

VOS Financial
415 Ave. D #106
Lake Charles, LA 70602
(send a #10 self-addressed
stamped envelope for quick reply.)

People's Financial
Route 1, Box 66
Crossett, AR 71635

Mason Finance Service
811 Manatee West
Bradenton, FL 33505

Mr. Jack Hessley
Hessley Currency Service, Unltd.
56 West Main St.
Geneva, OH 44041

O.S. Cater Agency
1635 Broadway
Lubboch, TX 79408

Gray Co Financial
405 Sunset Drive
Johnson City, TN 37601

Radcliff Associates
Dept. 5, GPO Box 1815
Brooklyn, NY 11202
(student loans and financial aid)

E. Golden
1840 Taft St.
Hollywood, FL 33020

Sunnyvale International
2627 19th St.
Rockford, IL 61109
(business and personal loans)

ARAB MONEY SOURCES

ALGERIA

Banque Centrale D'El-Djazair
(Central Bank)
8 Boul, Zirout-Youcef

Banque Exterieur D'El-Djazair
11 Boul. Col. Amirouche
El-Djazair
Tel: 611252
Telex: 52736
Cable: Algerex

Banque Nationale D'El-Djazair
8 Boul. Che Guevara
El-Djazair
Tel: 620530
Telex: WATANI

Credit Populaire D'El-Djazair
2 Boul. Col. Amirouche
Tel: 632855
Telex: 52512
Cable: CREPOPAL

BAHRAIN

Baharain Monetary Agency
(Central Bank)
PO Box 27, Manama
Tel: 241241
Telex: 8295 BRNBAK GJ
Cable: Naked Al Bahr

The Chartered Bank Ltd.
PO Box 29, Manama
Tel: 255933
Telex: 8229 CHARTABANK

Bank of Bahrain and Kuwait
PO Box 597, Manama
Tel: 253388
Telex: 8919/8284 UBK/GJ
Cable: BAHKUBAND BAHRAIN

The Arab Bank Ltd.
PO Box 813, Manama
Tel: 257981
Telex: 8647/8657
Cable: BANKARABI

Bank Melli Iran
PO Box 785, Manama
Tel: 259910-9
Telex: 8266 BKMELI GJ
Cable: BANKMELLIBAHRAIN

Banque du Caire
PO Box 815, Manama
Tel: 254454/254464
Telex: 8298 BCAIRE GJ
Cable: BANQUECAIRE

The British Bank of
the Middle East
PO Box 57, Manama
Tel: 255932
Telex: 8230 BBME GJ
Cable: CHARTABANK

First National City Bank
PO Box 548, Manama
Tel: 257 124
Telex: 8225 CITIB GJ
Cable: CITIBANK

The Chase Manhatten Bank N.A.
PO Box 368, Manama
Tel: 251401
Telex: 8286 CMBAH GJ
Cable: CHAMANBANK

Grindlays Bank Ltd.
PO Box 5793, Manama
Tel: 259641
Telex: 8220 GJ
Cable: Minerva Bahrain

Habib Bank (Overseas) Ltd.
PO Box 566, Manama
Tel: 255062
Telex: 9948 BNGJ
CABLE: HABIBANK

Rafidain Bank
PO Box 607, Manama
Tel: 255389
Telex: 5656/5456
Cable: UNITED

EGYPT

Central Bank of Egypt
(Central Bank)
31 Sharia Kasr El Nil, Cairo
Tel: 751529/751738/751541
Telex: 92237
Cable: MARKAZI

Arab African Bank
PO Box 5 Midan Al-Saray
Al-Koubru
Tel: 916744
Telex: Not available
Cable: ARABAFRO

Arab International Bank
(Foreign Trade & Development)
25 Sharia al del Khalek Sarwat St.
PO Box 1563, Cairo
Tel: 918794/916120
Cable: ARAKARI CAIRO

Bank of Alexandrai
(Manufacturing)
6 Sharia Salah Salam St.,
Alexandrai

Tel: 806212
Telex: 54107
Cable: HEADALEX

Banque Du Caire
22 Adly St., PO Box 1494, Cairo
Tel: 49446
Telex: 2022
Cable: BANKAHER

Banque Misr (Home Trade and
Agricultural Finance)
151 Mohamed Farid St., Cairo
Tel: 917455
Telex: 9224226
Cable: Cario

Egyptian General Agricultural
and Co-Operative Organization
Misr Insurance Building
Midan El-Guiza, Cairo
Tel: 897308
Telex: None
Cable: TASLIF

IRAN

Central Bank Markazi Iran
Ferdowsi Ave
Tehran
Tel: 310100-9
Telex: 21 3965-8
Cable: INTMELLAT

Bank Nationale De Paris
PO Box 490
Tehran
Tel: 842676
Telex: 213380 B Noir
Cable: NATIOPAR

IRAN

Barclays
Corner Ave. Forsat/Ayatollah
Taleghani
Tehran
Tel: 825074-5
Telex: 215005 BART

GET A CASH LOAN FROM YOUR STATE

Your state and many cities and county governments loan money at low interest rates for long periods of time. Generally, the restriction on these loans is that the money must be used to start or expand a business which offers jobs to people in the state community. These are the industrial development boards I mentioned in Volume One.

How to get a State or Local Loan

1. Have a good purpose for the loan.
2. Decide how much money is needed.
3. Prepare a pro-forma statement of proposed expansion plans.
4. Give a summary of your business experience for previous three years.
5. Have at least three personal and three business references.
6. List all the advantages your business will provide the state and/or community: a—number of jobs your business will provide; b—Average weekly payroll; c—Estimated net yearly profit; d—Educational and on-job training benefits for employees; e—Projections of future production.
7. List exactly how and where money will be spent.
8. Contact the agency itself for personal guidance on preparing your proposal.

To apply for a loan, simply call or write the agency in your state and request a loan application. They'll send the application within a few days. (Some state agencies may only lend to out-of-state businesses planning a move into the state).

Alabama Department of Economic
and Community Affairs
3455 Norman Bridge Rd.
Montgomery, AL 36105
(205) 261-2500

Alaska Dept. of Commerce
and Economic Development
PO Box D
Juneau, AK 99811
(907) 465-2500

Arizona Community Development
Dept. of Commerce
1700 W. Washington
West Wing 4th floor
Phoenix, AZ 85007
(602) 255-5434

Arkansas Industrial
Development Commission
#1 Capitol Mall
Little Rock, AR 72201
(501) 682-1121

California Dept. of Finance
1025 P St.
Sacramento, CA 95814
(916) 445-3878

Colorado Division of
Commerce and Development
1313 Sherman
Denver, CO 80203

Connecticut Economic
Development
Dept. 210 Washington St.
Hartford, CT 06106
(203) 566-3787

Delaware State Development Dept.
99 Kings Highway
PO Box 1401
Dover, DE 19903
(302) 736-4271

Florida Commerce Dept.
Bureau of Industrial Development
107 West Gaines St. Suite G-34
Tallahassee, FL 32399-2000
(904) 488-9360

Georgia Department
of Industry and Trade
PO Box 1776
Atlanta, GA 30301
(404) 656-3545

Hawaii Department of
Planning and Economic
Development
415 S. Beretania St.
Honolulu, HI 96813

Idaho Statehouse
700 West State St.
Boise, ID 83720

Illinois Board of Economic
Development
State Capitol Complex
401 S. Spring St.
Springfield, IL 62706

Indiana Department of Commerce
State House
200 W. Washington St.
Indianapolis, IN 46024

Iowa Development Commission
State Capitol
1007 E. Grand Ave.
Des Moins, IA 50319

Kansas Department of
Economic Development
State Capitol 2700 SW 6th. Ave.
Topeka, KS 66606

Kentucky Department of Revenue E.
Frankfort, KY 40620

Louisiana Department of
Commerce and Industry
State Capitol 900 Riverside St. N.
Baton Rouge, LA 70804

Maine Department of
Commerce and Development
79 Sewall St.
Augusta, ME 04330
(207) 626-3448

Maryland Department of
Economic Development
95 Calvert St.
Annapolis, MD 21401
(301) 974-2700

Massachusetts Department of
Commerce and Development
State Office Building
100 Cambridge St.
Boston, MA 02202

Michigan Department of
Business Expansion
Commerce Center
300 S. Capitol Ave.
Lansing, MI 48926

Minnesota Department of
Business Development
Dept. Of Commerce 8 4th. St. E
St. Paul, MN 55101

Mississippi Agricultural and
Industrial Board
515 E. Amite St.
Jackson, MS 39201

Missouri Department of
Economic Development
Truman Office Building
301 W. High St. Rm. 770
Jefferson City, MO 65105

Montana Economic Development
1520 E. 6th. Rm. 50
Helena, MT 59620

Nebraska Division of Resources
State Office 301 Centennial Mall
Lincoln, NE 68509

Nevada Dept. of Economic
Development
State Industrial Commission
Carson City, NV 89714

New Hampshire Division of
Economic Development
State House Annex
25 Capitol St.
Concord, NH 03301

New Jersey Division of
Economic Development
Trenton, NJ 08625

New Mexico Department
of Development
1100 St. Francis St.
Joseph M. Montoya Bldg.
Santa Fe, NM 87503
(505) 827-0300

New York Bureau Of
Industrial Development
Empire St. Plaza 1
Albany, NY 12227

North Carolina Commerce
and Industry Division
Department of Commerce
430 Salisbury St. N.
Raleigh, NC 27603

Ohio Development Department
State Office 65 S. Front St.
Columbus, OH 43215

Oklahoma Department of
Commerce and Industry
State Capitol
2300 N. Lincoln Blvd.
Oklahoma City, OK 73105

Oregon Department of Commerce
1400 SW 5th Ave.
Portland, OR 97201

Pennsylvania Bureau Of
Industrial Development
Dept. Of Revenue
Finance Harrisburg, PA 17127

Rhode Island Industrial
Building Authority
State Office 101 Smith St.
Providence, RI 02903

South Carolina State Development
Board State House
1100 Gervais St.
Columbia, NC 29201

South Dakota Industrial
Development Expansion Agency
State Office Building
Pierre, SD 57537

Tennessee Division for
Industrial Development
State Capitol Bldg.
600 Charlotte Ave. 37219

Texas Industrial Commission
Sam Houston State Office Building
201 E. 14th St.
Austin, TX 78701

Utah Industrial and
Employment Planning
State Capitol
Salt Lake City, UT 84114

Vermont Development
Department
Industrial Division
Montpelier, VT 05603

Virginia Division of
Industrial Planning
State Finance
1322 E. Grace St.
Richmond, VA 23219

Washington Department Of
Commerce and Development
Industrial Development Division
Washington State Agencies
Oylmpia, WA 98504

West Virginia Industrial
Development Div.
State Capitol
1800 Washington St. E.
Chaleston, WV 25305

Wisconsin Department of
Resource Development
State Office
201 E. Washington Ave. 53702

SECTION SEVEN

HOW TO BECOME A CORPORATE PRESIDENT IN THREE WEEKS

The decision on whether to incorporate an existing business, or a new one, is a big step and should be taken only after consulting with your accountant and attorney. Most businesses can benefit from incorporating, and it is not very difficult to do. In fact, you can do it yourself for under $100.

Although a corporation has certain disadvantages over a sole proprietorship or partnership form of business, the advantages far outweigh any disadvantages. For example, here are some of the benefits of incorporating:

1. Limited Liability—a corporation is considered a legal 'entity' in the eyes of the state. It can enter into contracts; it can sue or be sued. (If you are an owner or officer of a corporation, you cannot be personally sued for corporate debts.

2. Capital raising is easier with a corporate set-up. Any properly formed corporation can sell stocks or bonds to raise money.

3. Corporations enjoy certain tax breaks that regular businesses do not. It can also be used to provide the officers with medical, life, disability, and retirement benefits via corporate tax deductions.

4. A corporation does not "die" when its owner dies, as is the case with a regular business or partnership.

HOW TO FORM YOUR OWN CORPORATION

The basic procedure of incorporating consists of filling out and filing a Certificate of Incorporation in the state in which you select. You can incorporate in any state you like! You don't necessarily have to incorporate in your home state. In fact, there are distinct advantages to not doing so.

For example, the State of Delaware gives preferential treatment to corporations and accounts: more than one third of all corporations listed on the American and New York Stock Exchange are incorporated there.

In Delaware you can issue 'no-par' stock which is restricted in most states. Many states also require a certain dollar amount of capitalization; some have restrictive "blue sky laws"; some states even require stockholders to be partially liable for wages of an employee; corporate debt, and so on. Some simply take too long to grant a charter. Almost none of these problems exist with a Delaware corporation.

I have included actual forms which you can use to form your own corporation. One of these forms is the type issued by the state of Delaware, and the other has been adapted from it for use in your own state. Check with the Secretary of State on the appropriateness of the adapted form before filing.

Usually a corporation is composed of three people—a president, a secretary, and a treasurer. These can be friends or relatives. If you form a Delaware corporation, one person can hold all three offices.

In Delaware you also have the option of forming a corporation anonymously. One way to do this is by registering and using a fictitious name in your own state prior to filing. The other way is to have another corporation own the first one.

Most of the pornography stores are owned anonymously to prevent prosecution of the owners, and they employ entire "strings" of corporations—each owning another—with addresses leading through a maze of mail drops in distant cities. Big time operators also 'launder' their money in this manner and avoid paying income taxes as well.

To incorporate in Delaware, you must have a registered agent who files the papers for you and provides you with a business address in that state. Their address is then the legal address of your corporation. Some of the following firms charge under $150 for filing your articles of incorporation. To that figure, however, you must also add about $60 which will go to the state for filing fees, state tax, and for copies of the certificate. Thus, it is possible to incorporate for under $200. Write to some of the firms listed below for more information.

The Company Corporation
Wilmington, DE
(302) 575-0440

Corporate Agents
PO Box 1281
Wilmington, DE 19899
(302) 998-0598

Delaware Charter Co.
PO Box 8963
Wilmington, DE 19899
(302) 995-2131

Prentice-Hall Corp. System
Dover, DE 19903
(302) 674-1221

When submitting your certificate of incorporation for acceptance by the state, it is a good idea to list several names for your corporation in order of preference. If a name is all ready taken by another corporation, you can't use it.

CERTIFICATE OF INCORPORATION
OF

_____

First — The name of this corporation is _____

Second — Its registered office in the state of Delaware is to be located at _____
_____ in the _____ , County of
_____ . The registered agent in charge thereof is
_____ at _____

Third — The nature of the business and, the objects and purposes proposed to be transacted, promoted and carried on, are to do any or all of the things herein mentioned, as fully and to the same extent as natural persons might or could do, and in any part of the world, viz:

> "The purpose of the corporation is to engage in any lawful act or activity for which corporations may be organized under the general Corporation law of Delaware.

Fourth — The amount of the total authorized capital stock of this corporation is _____
_____ Dollars ($) divided into _____
shares, of _____ Dollars ($) each.

Fifth — The name and mailing address of the incorporator is as follows:

NAME: ADDRESS:

Sixth — The powers of the incorporator are to terminate upon filing of the certificate of incorporation, and the name(s) and mailing address(es) of persons who are to serve as director(s) until the first annual meeting of stockholders or until their successors are elected and qualify are as follows:

NAME AND ADDRESS OF DIRECTOR(S)

Seventh — The Directors shall have power to make and to alter or amend the By-Laws; to fix the amount to be reserved as working capital, and to authorize and cause to be executed, mortgages and liens without limit as to the amount, upon the property and franchise of this corporation.

With the consent in writing, and pursuant to a vote of the holders of a majority of the capital stock issued and outstanding, the Directors shall have authority to dispose, in any manner, of the property of this Corporation.

The By-Laws shall determine whether and to what extent the accounts and books of this corporation, or any of them, shall be open to the inspection of the stockholders; and no stockholder shall have any right of inspecting any account, or book, or document of this Corporation, except as conferred by the Law or By-Laws, or by resolution of the stockholders.

Who signed and executed the foregoing Articles of Incorporation, and they did acknowledge that they signed the foregoing and that the facts therein stated are true and correct.

IN WITNESS WHEREOF, I have set my hand and official seal this _____
day of _____ 19 _____ .

USE THIS FORM TO INCORPORATE IN
THE STATE OF DELAWARE ONLY

(Signature of person named in Fifth Article or signature of officer of corporation named in Fifth Article.)

_____

Notary Public, State and County aforesaid. My commission expires:

_____

CERTIFICATE OF INCORPORATION
OF

_____

First — The name of this corporation is _____

Second — Its registered office in the state of _____ is to be located at
_____ in the _____,
County of _____. The registered agent in
charge thereof is _____ at _____

Third — The nature of the business and, the objects and purposes proposed to be transacted, promoted and carried on, are to do any or all of the things herein mentioned, as
fully and to the same extent as natural persons might or could do, and in any part of the
world, viz:

"The purpose of the corporation is to engage in any lawful act or activity for
which corporations may be organized under the general Corporation law of
_____ .

Fourth — The amount of the total authorized capital stock of this corporation is
_____ Dollars ($) divided into _____
shares, of _____ Dollars ($) each.
Fifth — The names and mailing addresses of each of the incorporator or incorporators
are as follows:

NAME   MAILING ADDRESSES

_____   _____
_____   _____
_____   _____

Sixth — The Directors shall have power to make and to alter or amend the By-Laws; to
fix the amount to be reserved as working capital, and to authorize and cause to be executed,
mortgages and liens without limit as to the amount, upon the property and franchise of this
Corporation.

With the consent in writing, and pursuant to a vote of the holders of a majority of the
capital stock issued and outstanding, the Directors shall have authority to dispose, in any
manner, of the property of this Corporation.

The By-Laws shall determine whether and to what extent the accounts and books of
this corporation, or any of them, shall be open to the inspection of the stockholders; and
no stockholder shall have any right of inspecting any account, or book, or document of
this Corporation, except as conferred by the Law or By-Laws, or by resolution of the
stockholders.

Who signed and executed the foregoing Articles of Incorporation, and they did ackno-
ledge that they signed the foregoing and that the facts therein stated are true and correct.

IN WITNESS WHEREOF, I have set my hand and official seal this _____
day of _____ 19 _____

USE THIS FORM TO INCORPORATE WITHIN
YOUR OWN STATE ONLY

_____
(Signature of person named in Fifth Article or
signature of officer of corporation named in
Fifth Article.)

_____
Notary Public, State and County aforesaid. My
commission expires:

_____
(Notarial Seal)

CORPORATION BY-LAWS

ARTICLE I. NAME AND LOCATION. The name of this corporation shall be _____ . Its principal office shall be located at _____ _____ in the City of _____, State of _____ . Other offices for the transaction of business shall be located at such other places as the Board of Directors may from time to time determine.

ARTICLE II. CAPITAL STOCK. The total authorized capital stock of this corporation shall be _____ shares of common stock of: (check applicable line) (and preferred stock, if any)

_____ a. No par
_____ b. Par value of $_____ .
_____ c. Preferred stock, as follows: _____

All certificates of stock shall be signed by the President and the Secretary and shall be sealed with the corporate seal.

Treasury stock shall be held by the corporation subject to the disposal of the Board of Directors, and shall neither vote nor participate in dividends.

The corporation shall have a first lien on all the shares of its capital stock, and upon all dividends declared upon the same, for any indebtedness of the respective holders thereof to the corporation.

Transfers of stock shall be made only on the books of the corporation; and the old certificate, properly endorsed, shall be surrendered and cancelled before a new certificate is issued.

In case of loss or destruction of a certificate of stock, no new certificate shall be issued in lieu thereof except upon satisfactory proof to the Board of Directors of such loss or destruction; and upon the giving of satisfactory security against loss to the corporation; any such certificate shall be plainly marked "Duplicate" upon its face.

ARTICLE III. STOCKHOLDERS' MEETINGS. An annual meeting of the stockholders shall be held at _____ o'clock _____ M. on the _____ day _____ each year, commencing on the _____ day of _____ 19 _____ , or if said date shall be a holiday, on the following day, at the principal office of the corporation. At such meeting the stockholders shall elect directors to serve until their successors are elected and qualified.

A special meeting of the stockholders, to be held at the same place as the annual meeting, may be called at any time whenever requested by stockholders holding a majority of the outstanding stock.

Unless prohibited by law, the stockholders holding a majority of the outstanding shares entitled to vote may, at any time, terminate the term of office of all or any of the directors, with or without cause, by a vote at any annual or special meeting, or by written statement, signed by the holders of a majority of such stock, and filed with the secretary or, in his absence, with any other officer. Such removal shall be effective immediately even if successors are not elected simultaneoulsy, and the vacancies on the Board of Directors shall be filled only by the stockholders.

Notice of the time and place of all annual and special meetings shall be given 10 days before the date thereof, except that notice may be waived on consent of stockholders owning the following proportion of the outstanding stock: (Check applicable line).

_____ a. A majority
_____ b. Two-thirds majority
_____ c. Three-fourths majority
_____ d. Other: _____

The President, or in his absence, the Vice-President, shall preside at all meetings of the stockholders.

At every meeting, each stockholder of common stock shall be entitled to cast one vote for each share of stock held in his name, which vote may be cast by him either in person, or by proxy. All proxies shall be in writing, and shall be filed with the Secretary and by him entered of record in the minutes of the meeting.

ARTICLE IV.   DIRECTORS.   The business and property of the corporation shall be managed by a board of not less than three or by an executive committee appointed by said board.

The regular meeting of the directors shall be held immediately after the adjournment of each annual stockholders' meeting. Special meetings of the board of directors may be called by the president.

Notice of all regular and special meetings shall be mailed to each director, by the Secretary, at least 10 days before each meeting, unless such notice is waived.

A quorum for the transaction of business at any meeting of the directors shall consist of a majority of the members of the board.

The directors shall elect the officers of the corporation and fix their salaries. Such election shall be held at the directors' meeting following each annual stockholders' meeting. Any officer may be removed, with or without cause, by vote of the direcrors at any regular or special meeting, unless such removal is prohibited by law.

Vacancies in the Board of Directors may be filled by the remaining directors at any regular or special meeting of the directors, except when such vacancy shall occur through removal by stockholders holding a majority of the outstanding shares, as hereinabove provided.

At each annual stockholders' meeting, the directors shall submit a statement of the business done during the preceding year, together with a report of the general financial condition of the corporation, and of the condition of its property.

ARTICLE V. OFFICERS. The officers of the corporation shall be President, a Vice-President, a Secretary, and a Treasurer (and, in the discretion of the directors, an assistant secretary), who shall be elected for a term of one year, and shall hold office until their successors are elected and qualified.

The President shall preside at all directors' and stockholders' meetings; shall sign all stock certificates and written contracts and undertakings of the corporation; and shall perform all such other duties as are incident to his office. In case of disability, or absence from the city, of the President, his duties shall be performed by the Vice-President, who shall have equal and concurrent powers.

The Secretary shall issue notice of all directors' and stockholders' meetings; shall attend and keep the minutes of such meetings; and shall perform all such other duties as are incident to his office. In case of disability or absence, his duties shall be performed by the assistant secretary, if any.

The Treasurer shall have custody of all money and securities of the corporation. He shall keep regular books of account and shall submit them, together with all his vouchers, receipts, records, and other papers, to the directors for their examination and approval as often as they may require; and shall perform all such other duties as are incident to his office.

ARTICLE VI. DIVIDENDS AND FINANCE. Dividends, to be paid out of the surplus earnings of the corporation, may be declared from time to time by resolution of the Board of Directors by vote of a majority thereof.

The funds of the corporation shall be deposited in such bank or banks as the directors shall designate, and shall be withdrawn only upon the check of the corporation, signed as the directors shall from time to time resolve.

ARTICLE VII. AMENDMENTS. Amendments to these By-Laws may be made by a vote of the stockholders holding a majority of the outstanding stock at any annual or special meeting, the notice of such special meeting to contain the nature of the proposed amendment.

We hereby adopt and ratify the foregoing By-Laws.

———————————————
———————————————
———————————————
———————————————

SECTION EIGHT

HOW TO FORM A NON-PROFIT CORPORATION OR ASSOCIATION

Why am I teaching you how to start a non-profit organization in a book about making profits? The answer lies in the subtle meaning of the term 'non-profit'.

Non-profit corporations and associations can make profits as long as none of the profits go to you or your member's benefit. YOUR SALARY is NOT part of the profits—it's simply an expense of operating. Therefore, as the director of such an organization, you can draw a generous salary (commensurate with your duties), obtain insurance benefits, no cost travel, complimentary auto use, and much more.

As an example, why not start a non-profit organization whose purpose is to feed and clothe orphan children; or start a social center for the elderly, or even form your own church or religious cult.

Furthermore, once you form your organization, you can legally solicit for donations of merchandise, food, clothing, money, or anything else related to your 'cause'. It's a great way to create a prestigious lifetime job for yourself.

One fellow in Atlanta started a non-profit firm for the purpose of doing "research on taxes". He lives in luxury on his organization's tax-free income from book sales and donations.

Clearly then, a non-profit organization is something to be desired a least as a sideline activity. Maybe you're an artist and wish to set up a non-profit organization to teach deprived youngsters to paint. You would be paid a salary for doing something you enjoy and would probably be doing on your own anyway.

Look at it this way: With today's income tax system, it is becoming increasingly difficult to prepare for one's future financial security. The question is how can one provide for future lean years when the government steals up to HALF your earned income? The answer is to set up you own tax-exempt organization which can receive the fruits of your labor and accumulate the capital TAX-FREE. With a non-profit set-up, your future earnings are guaranteed as long as you choose to remain the director of your organization.

Choosing The Organizational Structure

If you plan on building your organization into one that handles a large amount of money, then a non-profit corporation is what you need. If on the other hand, your activity will be on a small scale, then a simple association may be formed. To form an association, contact you're Secretary of State and ask if your state requires you to file articles and by-laws. Some states do not require such a filing and in these cases, forming an association is merely a matter of preparing a statement concerning what your association is, who its members are, etc., and having it notarized. Be sure you check with your local and state government concerning any regulations they may have pertaining to forming such an organization.

If you plan on soliciting for funds, check with your city, county, and state to determine what, if any, reporting or registration requirements are involved.

A form on the next page has been printed for your possible use in forming your non-profit corporation, but be sure to check with your state to see if it is acceptable. Contact the IRS to find out how to file for a tax exemption.

With good planning and the tremendous tax breaks involved, you could build a national or international organization which might rival the empires of Rev. Moon, Rev. Ike, Father Divine, the Rosicrucians, and others who have become rich and powerful through tax-exempt corporations.

CONFIDENTIAL DIRECTORY OF HIGH-DISCOUNT MERCHANDISE SOURCES

Wholesale Supply Sources

The H.M.S. Company
6 East North Ave.
Northlake, IL 60164

Lakeside Products Co.
6646 N. Western Ave.
Chicago, IL 60645

Cook Brothers, Inc.
240 N. Ashland
Chicago, IL 60607

The Wholesale Outlet
1 Interstate Ave.
Albany, NY 12205

Pioneer Trading Co.
3922 W. Irving Park Rd.
Chicago, IL 60618

Wheeler Watch Co.
275 State St.
Schenectady, NY 12301

Galaxy Electroncis
5300 21St. Ave.
Brooklyn, NY 11204

Anchor Specialties Co.
PO Box 3958
North Providence, RI 02911

Williamson International, Inc.
PO Box 6778
Reno, NV 89513

Fireside Treasures
1401-D East Maynard Rd.
Cary, NC 27511

Two Brothers, Inc.
1602 Locust St.
St. Louis, MO

A great source for wholesale directories and catalogs is the "Sutton Family Mailing list." Write for information: *The Sutton Family*, 11565 Ridgewood Circle North, Seminole, FL 33542. They list manufacturers of over 10,000 wholesale and retail items.

CHILDREN'S

Cotton Dreams
Dept. BH
PO Box 99
Sebastian, FL 32958
Short-sleeved baby shirts, kimonos, training pants and diapers, etc. Merchandise is half off retail.

The Young Idea Ltd.
Aylesbury
HP 202JA England
Schoolwear, cord jeans, pajamas, nightgowns, and baby rompers.

FAMILY

Bemidji Woolen Mills
PO Box 277
Bemidji, MN 56601
Outerwear—jackets and coats. Prices are about 15 percent lower than department store prices.

Custom Coat Company, Inc.
227 N. Washington St.
Berlin, WI 54923
Outerwear and various other leather accessories. Prices are at least 25 percent below retail.

D&A Merchandise Co.
Dept. BH
22 Orchard St.
New York, NY
Name-brand robes, underwear and lingerie. Discount is about 25 percent.

Handart Embroideries
Room #106
Ming Way Building
36 Queen's Road Central
Hong Kong
Clothing, linens and sheets. Prices are 30 to 80 percent below retail.

Icemart
PO Box 23
Keflavik International Airport
Iceland
Sweaters, jackets, and accessories knitted of Icelandic Lopi wool. The discount is about 30 percent below U.S. prices.

I. Tuschman & Sons, Inc.
61 Orchard St.
New York, NY 10002
Name-brand underwear, sleep-
ware, shirts, jeans, etc. Prices are
25 to 35 percent below retail.

Rammagerdin of Reykjavik
Hafnarstraeti 19
PO Box 751-121
Reykjavik, Iceland
Wool and fur products—50 per-
cent below retail.

Romenes-Paterson Ltd.
Edinborough Woolen
MillLangholm Dumfriesshier
Scotland DG130BR
Suits and Shetland sweaters.

MEN'S

The Deersking Place
283 Akron Rd.
Epharata, PA 17522
Jackets, coats, handbags, shoes,
etc.—30 to 50 percent off.

Jos. A. Bank Clothiers
109 Market Pl.
Baltimore, MD 21202
"Preppie-style" clothing at savings
of 25 to 30 percent.

WOMEN'S

Bra Bar
28 Cedarhurst Ave.
Cedarhurst, NY 11516
Ladies' name-brand lingerie and
bras are 25 to 50 percent off.

Chadwick's of Boston, Ltd.
One Chadwick Pl.
PO Box 1600
Brockton, MA 02403
Variety of clothing. The discount
is 20 to 40 percent off retail.

Dreamy Down Fashions
Suite 185, 287 W. Butterfield Rd.
Emhurst, Il 60126
This store sells clothing at 40 to
60 percent off retail prices.

Heband Co.
265 N. Ninth St.
Paterson, NJ 07530
Products made in the U.S.A.

Huntington Clothiers and
Shirtmakers
1285 Alum Creek Dr.
Columbus, OH 43209
The discount is about 30 to 40
percent.

D. MacGillivary & Co.
Western Isles, PA 888 5LA
Scotland Sweaters, knitwear at a
discount.

The Priscilla Co.
49 Alden St.
Fall River, MA 02723
Prices are 30 to 50 percent below
retail.

Royal Silk
Royal Silk Plaza
45 E. Madison Ave.
Clifton, NJ 07110
Prices are 40 percent less than
retail stores.

Saint Laurie Ltd.
897 Broadway
New York, NY 1003
This company hand-tailors items
and the discount is 30 to 50 percent below retail.

WHOLESALERS

Abbey Road Ltd.
1407 Broadway
New York, NY

B & F Manufacturing Ltd.
1411 Broadway
New York, NY

Barclay Square Inc.
1400 Broadway
New York, NY

Best of Friends
112 W. 34th
New York, NY

Brook House
232 Madison Ave.
New York, NY

Capriccio International Inc.
525 7th Ave.
New York, NY

Carlton Garment Co.
692 Broadway
New York, NY

Casey Manufacturing
132 W. 36th
New York, NY

Chic Togs Fashion
470 7th Ave.
New York, NY.

Cross Roads Mfg. Inc.
132 W. 39th
New York, NY

Daniel Laurent Ltd.
589 8th Ave.
New York, NY.

D&M sportswear Mfg. Co.
29 Allen
New York, NY

Deer Variety Fashions
31 Orchard
New York, NY

Daisy Sportswear Inc.
212 W. 35th
New York, NY

Ecobay Sportswear Inc.
1431 Broadway
New York, NY

Fire Islander Woman
1407 Broadway
New York, NY

G&C Creations Inc.
53 Orchard
New York, NY

Gailord Classics Inc.
1407 Broadway
New York, NY

Gina Originals
1359 Broadway
New York, NY

Harbour Road Inc.
1411 Broadway
New York, NY

Haymaker Sports Inc.
498 7th Ave.
New York, NY

Hazen Sportswear Co.
426 7th Ave.
New York, NY

Hi-Lite Sport & Knitwear Corp.
328 Grand
New York, NY

Ina Sportswear
20 W. 20th Ave.
New York, NY

Jonabarry Originals Inc.
525 7th Ave.
New York, NY

Klasssiks Ltd.
830 W. 34th
New York, NY

Lady Arrow
1407 Broadway
New York, NY

Lady Devon
1441 Broadway
New York, NY

Lido Sportswear
135 W. 50th
New York, NY

Mel Morton Inc.
525 7th Ave.
New York, NY

APPLIANCES

ABC Vacuum Warehouse
Dept. BH
6720 Burnet Rd.
Austin, TX 78575

Apni Dookan
42 East Canal St.
New York, NY 10002
Name-brand audio components at
a discount of 30 percent.

The Archer Ave. Store
4193 Archer Ave.
Chicago, IL 60632
This store carries a complete
selection of Sony blank tapes at a
discount of 30 percent.

Bernie's Discount Center
Dept. BH
821 6th Ave.
New York, NY 10001
Phone-answering machines,
calculators etc.

Bloom & Krup
206 First Ave.
New York, NY 10009
Appliances and bedding. Ten to
thirty percent discount.

Boardman, Ltd.
833 Broadway
Albany, NY 12201
Wide variety—adult games, yogurt makers, jewelry etc. Discounts up to 40 percent.

International Solgo of
Long Island, Inc.
1745 Hempstead Turnpike
Elmont, NY 11003
Appliances, audio components, cameras etc.

Jems Sounds
785 Lexington Ave.
New York, NY 10021
Name-brand audio and video equipment. Discounts 10 to 35 percent.

Kunst Sales
45 Canal St.
New York, NY 10021
Audio and video components, luggage up to 50 percent off retail.

LVT Price Quote Hotline
Dept. BH
PO Box 444
Commack, NY 11725

Sewin' in Vermont
84 Concord Ave.
St. Johnsbury, VT 05819
Name-brand sewing machines. Discounts are anywhere from 25 to 50 percent.

Sew 'n' Vac
82 E. Main St.
Newark, DE 19711

Sound Reproduction, Inc.
7 Industrial Rd.
Fairfield, NJ 07006
Audio equipement. Discounts to 30 percent.

Stereo Corp. of America
1629 Flatbush Ave.
Brooklyn, NY 11210

CAMERAS

Aerocomp, Ince
Redbird Airport, Building 8
PO Box 24829
Dallas, TX 75224

All Electronics Corp.
PO Box 20406
Los Angeles, CA 90006
This store sells surplus electronics.

Cambridge Camera Exchange Inc.
Seventh Ave. and 13th St.
New York, NY 10011
Cameras, lights and lenses are 30 to 50 percent less than retail.

Elek-Tek
6557 N. Lincoln Ave.
Chicago, IL 60645
Calculators, computers etc.—at least a 20 percent discount.

Etco
Route 90 9N
North Country Shopping Center
Plattsburgh, NY 12901
Non name-brand electronic parts. Discounts are 20 to 80 percent.

Executive Photo and Supply Corp.
120 W. 31st. St.
New York, NY 10001
Cameras, lenses, film, paper and
photographic accessories. Also
calculators, computers etc.

Fortune Star
12 West 23rd St.
New York, NY 10010

Focus Electronics
4523 13th Ave.
Brooklyn, NY 11219
Electronics, cameras, computers,
appliances, etc.

Garden Camera
345 7th Ave.
New York, NY 10001
Darkroom supplies, cameras,
videos, calculators and electronic
games, watches, computers and
telephones. Prices are 30 to 50
percent below retail.

J & R Music World
23 Park Row
New York, NY 10038
Computers, stereo equipment,
video recorders, cameras and
blank tapes etc.

Olden Camera
Dept. BH
1265 Broadway at 32nd. St.
New York, NY 10001
Slide projectors, meters, motors,
video equipment, electronics,
computers, business machines and
copying equipment as well as
name brand cameras.

Pan American Electronics, Inc.
1117 Conway
Mission, TX 78572
This company sells TVs, radios,
security systems and calculators.

Saverite Photo & Electronics
46 Canal St.
New York, NY 10002
Small appliances, silver, stereo
and video equipment, watches
and TV screens are 40 to 50 percent below retail.

Solar Cine Products
4247 S. Kedzie Ave.
Chicago, IL 60632
Film products and accessories.
Discounts are up to 40 percent.

Spiratone
Dept BH
135-06 Norther Blvd.
Flushing, NY 11354
Camera accessories.

Stereo Discounters Electronic World
6730 Santa Barbara Court
Baltimore, MD 98103
Audio and Video equipment at
discounts of 20 to 60 percent off
the manufacturer's suggested retail
price.

Telephones Unlimited
Dept BH
PO Box 1147
San Diego, CA 92112

FURNITURE

American Furniture Systems
805 Kings Highway
Brooklyn, NY 11223
Chairs, tables, bookcases, desks,
etc.

Annex Furniture Galleries
PO Box 958
High Point, NC 27261
Savings are 40 to 50 percent off
retail.

Bales Furniture Manufacturing
1300 17th St.
San Francisco, CA 94107
Beds, wall beds, chests, hutches,
cabinets, dressers and bookcases
are available at discount prices.

Country Workshop
95 Rome St.
Newark, NJ 07105
This company sells unfinished
bookcases, cabinets, chests, tables,
desks and beds at a discount of
about 50 percent.

King's Chandelier Company
PO Box 667
Eden, NC
Discounts are about 50 percent.

Loftin-Black Furniture Co.
941 Randolph St.
Thomasville, NC 27360
The savings are about 40 percent
below retail.

Murrow Furniture Galleries
PO Box 4337
Wilmington, NC 27360
This company sells the name-
brands at 30 to 50 percent below
retail.

Priba Furniture Sales
PO Box 13295
Greensboro, NC 27405

Rose Furniture CO.
Dept. BH
PO Box 1829
214 Elm St.
High Point, NC 27261
Name-brand furniture at up to 40
percent off.

Shaw Furniture Galleries
131 W. Academy St. 576 BH
Randleman, NC 27317
This store sells brass beds, clocks,
lamps, mirrors, bedding, lighting
and even grand pianos as well as
other furniture at up to 40 percent
off.

Sion Fuk Enterprises
125-2 Wu-Fu 2nd. Rd.
Kaohsiung, Taiwan
Republic of China
Rosewood, teak and camporwood
furniture. The discounts are 30 to
70 percent.

Sobol House
140 Richardson Blvd.
Black Mountain, NC 28711

Today's Furniture Gallery
208 E. Green Drive
High Point, NC 27260
Contemporary furniture. Prices are 35 to 45 percent below retail.

Utility Craft, Inc.
Route 1, Box 501
Willard Rd.
High Point, NC 27260
Solid wood furniture at a discount of 40 to 50 percent.

DO-IT-YOURSELF

Hobbies and Crafts

America's Hobby Center, Inc.
Dept Bh
146 W. 22nd St.
New York, NY 10011
This store sells kits for model airplanes, railroads, ships and cars. The discounts are 10 to 40 percent.

Berman Leathercraft
145 South St.
Boston, MA 02111
Lizard, snake, antelope and cowhide skins in addition to leather and suede.

Boycan's Craft and Art Supplies
Dept. Bh
PO Box 897
Sharon, PA 16146
Needlework, flower making, doll

making etc. Discounts are about 30 percent, and additional discounts are given for purchases of more than $25.

Clotilde
237 SW 28th St.
Ft. Lauderdale, FL 33315
Hard-to-find items for sewing, patterns, etc.

Conover Woodcraft Specialties
18125 Madison Rd.
Parkman, OH 44062
Joiners, bits, drills, planers, sanders and saws etc.

Columbus Clay Company
1331 Edgehill Rd.
Columbus, OH 43212
Ceramic supplies.

Craftsman Wood Service Co.
1735 W. Cortland Ct.
Addison, IL 60101
Tools at a discount.

Craft Basket
Colchester CT 06415
Kits for wooden biplanes, trains, tractor-trailers, race cars, doll cradles, tanks, wagons, rocking horses, etc.

Curriculum Resources, Inc.
Dept BH
PO Box 923
Fairfield, CT 006430
This store sells products for almost every craft. Savings are about 10 percent.

Cutter Ceramics
PO Box 151
Waltham, MA 02154

Dick Blick Creative Materials
PO Box 1267
Galesburg, IL 61401
Artist supplies.

Eagle Ceramics
12266 Wilkins Ave.
Rockville, MD 20852

Empire Models
PO Box 42287, Dept C
Tucson, AZ 85733
Radio-controlled model airplanes
and accessories.

Graphic Chemical & Ink Co.
728 N. Yale Ave.
PO Box 27
Villa Park, IL 60181
Materials for etching, lithography,
block printing and silk screening.
Prices are 25 to 40 percent below
competitors.

Grieger's, Inc.
Dept BH
900 South Arroyo Parkway
PO Box 93070
Pasadena, CA 91109
Jewelry design materials.

The Hobby Market
PO Box 2172
Fort Worth, TX 76113

New York Central Art Supply Inc.
62 Third Ave.
New York, NY 10003

Twenty percent below retail.
The Potter's Shop
34 Lincoln St.
Newton Highlands, MA 02161
This company sells potter's books
at 15 to 50 percent below retail.

Sculpture House
38 E. 30th
New York, NY 10016

Daniel Smith Inc.
4130 First Ave. South
Seattle, WA 98134
Oriental art supplies and print-
making equipment as well as
paints, pastels, canvas, paper,
brushes and calligraphy items.
This discount is 20 to 50 percent.

Squadron Mail-Order
1115 Crowley Dr.
Carrollton, TX 75011
Model airplanes, motorcycles,
bombers, battleships, tanks and
other 'militaria' have discounts of
30 to 70 percent off.

Thos. Manetta
61 Hoffman Ave.
Elmont, NY 11003
There are 20 to 30 percent discounts on name brand binoculars,
theater glasses, microscopes and
telescopes.

Westwood Ceramic Supply Co.
14400 Lomitas Ave.
City of Industry, CA 91744
This store sells clays, glazes, clay
mixers, wheels, tools, kilns and
books.

HOUSEWARES

A.B. Schou
4 NY Ostergrade
1101 Copenhagen Denmark
Saving are 30 percent off retail on name brands.

Albert S. Smyth Co., Inc.
Dept BH
25 W. Aylesbury Rd.
Timonium, MD 21093
China, crystal, jewelry and gifts are sold by this company at savings of 25 to 50 percent.

American Archives
Dept BH
5535 N. Long Ave.
Chicago, IL 60630
Sterling silver is this company's specialty with prices 25 to 75 percent below retail.

Ben Morris Jewelry Co.
Dept. Bh
PO Box 7305
4417 Lovers Lane
Dallas TX 75209
This company carries fine lines of sterling silver, stainless flatware, silverplate holloware, china, crystal, diamonds and watches.

Bradley's
PO Box 1300
Columbus, GA 31993
Barbecue grills and equipment for cooking with charcoal or gas are discounted 15 to 50 percent.

Carl's House of Silver
86 W. Palisade Ave.
Dept BH
Englewood, NJ 07631
Silver, gold, flatware, jewelry, and other fine giftware are 20 to 50 percent off retail prices.

The Chef's Catalog
3915 Commercial Ave.
Northbrook, IL 60062
Cookware items. Discounts range to 40 percent.

The Chef's Warehouse
PO Box M
Montpelier, VT 05602
Cookware items at discounts of up to 20 percent.

Chinacraft of London
Parke House
130 Barlby Rd.
London W10 6BW, England
Discounts are up to 50 percent.

The China Closet
6807 Wisconsin Ave.
Bethesda, MD 20815

The China Warehouse
PO Box 5205
Akron, OH 4313

Feldman Brothers
1954-58 Third Ave.
New York, NY 10029
This company carries dinnerware, pottery, porcelain, and wall coverings.

Grand Finale
PO Box 819027
Farmers Branch, TX 75381
Designer clothing, fine furnishing
and elegant accessories are sold
here at discounts of 40 to 50 percent off.

Greater New York Trading Co.
Dept BH
81 Canal St.
New York, NY 10002
Discounts of 40 to 60 percent can
be found here on tableware.

Haruta & Co., Inc.
150 5th Ave.
New York, NY 10010

Imoco Inc.
3225 Premier
PO Box 152052
Irving, TX 75063
Housewares.

International Housewares
PO Box 1826
Pittsfield, MA 01202

J. Schachter Corp.
115 Allen St.
New York, NY 10202
Comforters, pillows, linens and
towels etc.

Just-Irv Wicker
25 Renwick St.
New York, NY 12550

Kitchen Bazaar
Dept BH
4455 Connecticut Ave.
Washington D.C. 20008
Discounts of up to 70 percent.

The Kippen Group
Dept. BH
102 Dal-Rick Village
Richardson, TX 75080
Name brand china and crystal are
up to 50 percent below retail
prices.

Missina Glass & China Co.
Route 30
Elwood, NJ 08217
Discounts of 30 to 70 percent.

Quiltessence
133 Eldridge St.
New York, NY 10002
Down-filled comforters, pillows
and sheets.

Reject China Shop
33-34-35 Beauchamp PL.
London SW3 1NU
England
China settings and porcelain are
this company's specialty. Name
brands are discounted 15 to 50
percent.

Robin Importers
510 Madison Ave.
New York, NY 10022
This company has a large variety
of stainless steel, china cutlery,
crystal, giftware, bakeware, and
tablecloths.

Rogers & Rosenthal, Inc.
105 Canal St.
New York, NY 10013
Name-brand Glassware, china,
crystal and flatware at 65 percent
off retail.

Rubin & Green
290 Grand St.
New York, NY 10002
Bed and table linens.

Saxkjaers
53 Kobmagergade
1150 Copenhagen K
Denmark
Porcelain collector's plates at 40 percent below U.S. retail.

Weston Bowl Mill
Main St. Route 100
Weston, VT 05161
Wooden household and kitchen items.

JEWELRY

BMI
1617 Promenade Bank Building
Richardson, TX 75080
Gold Chains at up to 50 percent off.

Crown Cultured Pearl Corp.
580 8th Ave.
New York, NY 10018
Gemstones, such as jade, coral,onyx, malachite and carnelians. The discount is 20 to 60 percent.

Empire Diamond Corp.
Dept BH
Empire State Building
66th floor 350 5th Ave.
New York, NY 10010

Hasco Industries, Inc.
135 5th Ave.
New York, NY10010
This company sells costume jewelry, genuine diamonds, stone pendants, necklaces and earrings.

Helen Jewelry Co. Inc.
15 West 47th St.
New York, NY 10036
This company sells 14K chains, bracelets, charms, earrings and rope chains.

House of Onyx
Dept. BH
#1 North Main
The Rowe Building
Greenville, KY 42345
This company sells loose diamonds, opals, sapphires, emeralds, tiger-eye, malahite and blue topaz at 50 percent off.

Love's
2030 Cherry Rd.
Rock Hill, SC 29731
Fine jewelry such as necklaces, earrings and bracelets made from pearls, onyx, laiz ameathyst, rubies, sapphires, diamonds, emeralds and sterling silver. Prices are between 20 to 50 percent below retail.

M & I Haaberman Inc.
Dept. BH
380 Lexington Ave., Suite 521
New York, NY 10168
Fine jewelry and name brand watches are 25 to 35 percent below retail.

Rama Jewelry Ltd.
OPP Rama Tower Hotel
987 Silom Rd.
Bangkok, Thailand
This company sells gems, jewelry,
Thai silks, silverware, bronze
ware, leather goods, teakwood
carvings and other local products.

Rennie Ellen
15 W. 47th St. #401
New York, NY 10036
This wholesale diamond company
sells their products at up to 75
percent off.
Vanity Fair
55E. Washington St.
Chicago, IL 60602

FIREARMS

Here are two gun and ammuni-
tion wholesalers where you can
buy your products and make huge
profits. In Volume 3 I will be going into much greater detail as to
how you can make money selling
guns.

AJ Wholesale Guns
1944 W. Ridge Rd.
Rochester, NY 14626

B & B Sales
11100 Cumpston St.
N. Hollywood, CA 91601

New Books &
Moneymaking
Opportunities

Cash in On
Government Money

Need to get grants and loans, but just don't know where to turn? Have you tried the federal government? That's right, the federal government has many programs that can result in your getting money few people know about. Get money for education, business, houses and more. This book shows you what these programs are and where to go to take advantage of them. In addition to the checks that can come your way from the government, you will learn how you can get houses, appliances, cars and even businesses from the government at rock bottom prices! Find out how to get government money just for filling out a few forms in *Cash in on Government Money*.   #5033 $10

The Self-Publishers
Opportunity Kit

The Self-Publisher's Opportunity Kit contains eight interesting books—they've all been tested and are proven sellers. Each book comes with a copyright agreement, which allows you to reprint and sell as many copies as you wish, and complete, step-by-step instructions on how to market these books for the greatest profit.

In addition to the eight titles, you get proven-effective classified ads and a sales letter to promote your books. Some of the books measure 24, 8½-by-11-inch pages.

The eight books are:
1. How To Get Free Grants
2. Importing—Your Key To Success
3. Making A Fortune With Real Estate
5. The Secret Of Raising Money
6. The Millionaire's Secret Of Growing Rich
7. How To Influence People And Win Them Over
8. How To Get $200,000 In Benefits From The U.S. Gov't

The Self-Publisher's Opportunity Kit, with eight books, certificate of reprint rights, step-by-step instructions, sales letter and classified ads, is only $25.   #1633

Getting Anything You Want Absolutely Free or Next to Nothing

Can you imagine having free products sent to you everyday? It's possible with this system I've developed. In addition, you can pay pennies on the dollar for almost anything. It's yours just for the asking. This includes jewelry, designer clothing, automobiles, stereo and electronic equipment and cameras. This book shows you how and where to get them and then turn around and sell them for a fantastic profit. It tells you how to buy goods at auctions, bankruptcies and closeouts where your cost can be just 10 cents to the dollar.

Once you start finding these bargains, your friends will be stalking you to get these outrageously low prices for them. They will know they have been paying five and ten times what you are paying for the very same thing. #4733 $10

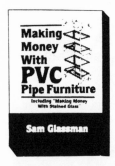

$10,000 a Month Making PVC Furniture

Sam Glassman

There is big money to be made in PVC furniture. All you need to make beautiful, profit-making furniture is a hacksaw, pencil, tape measure, glue and some of your spare time. Here is what is included in your book:

• Where you can buy PVC pipe wholesale
• Detailed, easy-to-follow plans of the hottest-selling furniture
• A complete marketing plan that will show you how to sell your furniture to anxious buyers
• How to make up to $100 an hour with these easy-to-assemble furniture pieces.
• Photographs and step-by-step instructions

The craze is on. PVC furniture that never needs painting is commanding high prices at your local furniture stores. Not only are people buying this non-corroding, sturdy furniture for outdoors, but interior designers are recommending its use indoors. You can make a lot of money in this hot new business with this complete guide to PVC furniture. #2933 $7

Seeing Through Anyone

Tom Foster

Two hundred dollars can be yours in just 15 minutes by reading people instantly through their handwriting. You will learn how to read into someone's mind through their handwriting; they will be so amazed they will pay your price and refer you to all their friends. It's easy and effective. If you can tell the difference between a straight line and a loop, you are on your way to making thousands of dollars! It's that easy and it's guaranteed. People will gladly pay you hundreds of dollars to understand themselves. With this type of potential, how can they refuse?

0533 $10.00

The Complete Credit Book

Get out from under unwanted debts, clear up your financial picture and get that credit you want and need, including a VISA and/or Mastercard. This is for anyone who wants to know how to straighten out his or her financial situation, or who just wants to get better credit. Learn how the creditors work on you and how you can be rid of them. Also find out what types of credit you can get and how each system works. Here's a very factual, knowledgeable and realistic guide to getting credit, including the usually hard to obtain credit cards. Even if you have some credit, you may not know what your rights are and how you can improve your financial picture; wonder no more and read all about it. #5233 $15

How to Make a Fortune Writing and Selling Information by Mail

David Buckley

This manual by David Buckley tells you how to get into the mail order business. His tips and secrets make it plain how easy it is to make money from writing information. Never written before? This book shows how easy it really is. Don't know what kind of books will sell? This book reveals what types of information will do well. Not sure how selling by mail works? This manual will reveal all you need to know. Short on funds? This books shows you how to minimize your expenses, while greatly expanding your profits. It's amazing how valuable information can be, and how you can profit on its worth. And when you have someone as experienced as David Buckley as a guide, then you will be on the 'write' track to making your fortune through selling information by mail. $10
#3533

Unique Packages

Pete Branin

Discover the joys of giving away unique packages. That's right, you can make money by giving away unique packages. These are packages that people want. They will be very happy to receive them from you, and you will be happy to give them away because you know they will make you money. Find out how this unique system works and what is in it for you. You can make a lot of money, more than you may have imagined, just for giving away these packages. So few people are offering this service that now is the time to find out how to get in on this unique package giveaway. This remarkable method is like no other money-making plan you have ever seen in your life. It will make the American dream a reality for you. Find out how it works. See the benefits people will get from these packages; see how easy it is, and, best of all, see how you can make money off this unique system merely for giving away unique packages. $10
#1333

Making $500,000 a Year in Mail Order

David Bendah

If you ever dreamed of having your mailbox crammed with thousands of envelopes each containing a check in your name, working any hours you want, whenever you want, and being able to afford the pleasures life has to offer in one of this country's most lucrative businesses, then this book can make those dreams a reality.

Many people, including the author, have made a lot of money in mail order. Mail order is one of the most lucrative businesses you can get involved in. Work in your home, part-time if you want, to realize your life-long dreams of security.

Bendah's book is full of helpful, easy-to-understand information. Bendah, considered one of the nation's leading ad writers, teaches laymen how best to use his unique techniques and explains every aspect of book formation and marketing. He even goes so far as to print his confidential ad results from the many successful mail order ads he has run. He discloses his secret formula that has ensured the success of many mail order businesses. If you ever had a dream of making it big in mail order, *Making $500,000 A Year In Mail Order* can be your key. #1233 $15

Home Business Opportunities

Russ von Hoelscher

Small business/home business authority Russ von Hoelscher offers you scores of new, dynamic, unusual and proven ways to make lots of money in the comfort of your own home. In home. In addition to almost 100 home business moneymaking plans (most of which can be started with little or no investment), there are in-depth sections on making money in mail order and how to prosper as an information-age "how-to" author and/or publisher.

Take advantage of this volume so that you can make money at home. This informative, 365-page book lets you stay home and be a moneymaking success. #0877 $15

Free Grants
& Low-Interest Loans

Lloyd Sanders

Have you ever wondered how people with credit ratings lower than yours obtain money? The only difference between them and you is that they know how and where to get the money. Every year billions of dollars are given to people just like you. Would you like to stake your share? You can, by owning one of the most complete books on money-financing systems. It shows you how to get money from almost every possible source available. Hundreds of methods of raising money are covered in this book.

- Get up to $500,000 in easy-to-qualify SBA loans
- Get up to $350,000 if you're in business and handicapped
- Get up to $315,000 in low-income assistance
- Raise $50,000 with no collateral
- Borrow up to $100,000 from any commercial bank
- Raise up to $50,000,000 the corporate way
- Get up to $67,000 for a home purchase
- Get up to $5,000 a year for education
- Get up to $92,000 for home improvements
- Get up to $150,000 if you are a woman in business
- Learn loopholes in bank policies
- Use creative financing to raise large amounts of capital
- Use advanced banking techniques to get loans
- 270 foundations that will give you a free grant
- Get some of the $3 billion given out by foundations every year
- Get money from 300 financial institutions that loan by mail

These are just some of the money-raising techniques included. *Free Grants & Low-Interest Loans* must contain almost every known method of raising money. Each 5½-by-8½-inch book is $7   #0633

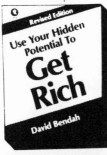

How to Use Your Hidden
Potential to Get Rich

David Bendah

This book presents a program that clearly maps the route self-made millionaires took to make their fortunes. Any very successful person who has made millions has used the techniques in this book.

Hidden Potential will show any individual, regardless of skill, intelligence and experience, how to use the mind to realize both business and personal dreams.

A complete success program, it is illustrated with charts and diagrams that enable understanding of the mind-transformation process. Included are quizzes that monitor the reader's progress to wealth. David Bendah, the author, backs up his points with interesting examples of how ordinary people—from Milton Hershey to William Colgate—used the same techniques to make fortunes. Bendah also devotes three chapters to Japanese wealth-building techniques. In short, this volume is designed to expose the reader to every success principle needed to get rich. #0433 $12

The $25 Billion Treasure

David Bendah

Right now there are billions of dollars that the states are holding for people entitled to it. By helping these people get the money from the states, you can profit. Find out here, in a complete book that explains what unclaimed money is and how you can profit from it. This book shows you how the states operate and how to take advantage of this when looking for unclaimed money. Looking at this book, you will be amazed at how much money there is out there and how easy it is for you to take advantage of it. It's incredible, but many states don't do a good job of finding these people. And why should they? After all, the state gets to gain interest on the money while they hold it. You, on the other hand, can get the money to the rightful heirs and, at the same time, help yourself to your fair share for your efforts. This book will leave you wide-eyed with amazement when you discover how unclaimed money can benefit you! #3633 $25

How to Get Rich in Mail Order

Melvin Powers

You can learn what to do and what not to do in starting your own mail order business from the voice of experience—Melvin Powers, a book publisher and mail order entrepreneur, who has worked in this profitable business for over 25 years. In this volume he shares what he has learned and can help make you successful in this field. Powers shows you how to be creative and, thus, profitable. This book shows you strategies for success, along with practical advice on marketing, advertising and finding a product and service to sell. It is full of samples and examples, so it is easy to learn from this book. Additionally, the book tells you how to sell products on television. The variety of subjects covered makes this a valuable reference source for the person interested in the mail order business. $20
#2655

Thousands of Dollars a Day With Your Camera

Jeff Peters

How would you like to get paid $100 for each picture you take? You don't even have to be a skilled photographer. Take ten pictures an hour and put $1000 in your pocket. Imagine becoming financially independent with this revolutionary method of making money with a camera. If you own any type of camera, you can put this plan into effect immediately. Thousands of dollars can be yours for only taking some snapshots. You don't have to know how to develop film, you don't need a darkroom and you don't really need to know anything about photography. Here is a business you can set up right away.

As soon as you receive this book, you can be making thousands of dollars a day. All you need to do is aim your camera, take the picture and the money is yours. #2733 $12.95

Get Rich with No Work

David Holmes & Joel Andrews

You can get rich without working by using the multi-level approach. Let me explain it. Your agents get the product from the company, but you get the commission from your agents and each agent they enlist. Others do the work while you sit back and collect the high commissions. Thousands of people just like you are making more than $100,000 a year without working. Once you have this book you can begin to create your fortune with any product you choose.

Holmes and Andrews, the authors, have a combined 20 years of sales and marketing experience. Holmes, a marketing expert and author of two books, has made more than 150 television and radio appearances over the past year. Andrews, who has personally launched six successful business ventures, is so highly regarded in sales and marketing that he has testified on marketing to both Houses of Congress. Together, these men teach you how to get rich without working. #1855 $15

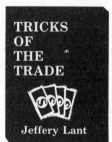

Tricks Of The Trade
Jeffery Lant

A penny for your thoughts? Why not make big money selling your advice? Here's how. TRICKS OF THE TRADE is the complete guide to succeeding in the advice business, written by the king of consultanting, Dr. Jeffery Lant. Use this book to obtain clients and effectively give them the advice they need. TRICKS OF THE TRADE is about more than selling your time. It teaches a revolutionary approach to giving advice professionally. It involves "a 10-part wealth-producing machine based on information processes you have at your disposal." And with TRICKS OF THE TRADE at your disposal you can help others, control your life's destiny,and produce a healthy profit for yourself.$30 #5533

How To Achieve Total Success

Jeffery Lant

An Owner's Manual for rich, loving, creative, healthy, happy and powerful living. Open your heart to unconditional love, your mind to new awareness, your body to better health and your wallet to ever-increasing wealth. #0933 $15

$2,000 an Hour

David Bendah

Would you like $2,000 for just making a few phone calls and looking in a few directories? That is all you have to do to enjoy this kind of money. If you can read English and can talk on the phone, you will be able to make thousands of dollars in a few hours.

One out of 10 Americans owns unclaimed property worth $325 billion. This amount increases by $1 billion every year. These people have forgotten or lost their money in bank accounts, stocks and unclaimed insurance policies. The states make no real effort to contact these money owners. Why should they, when unclaimed property is one of their biggest sources of revenue, second only to taxes?

As soon as you receive this book, you could make up to $2,000 an hour. All you need is a phone and a telephone book. This proven ingenious system in this book can be learned in one half hour. After that, you are all set. If you can read English and can talk on the phone, you could be making $2,000 an hour. $12.95
#0733

Make a Fortune & Travel Absolutely Free

Ben & Nancy Dominitz

Have you heard about the fat commission checks and free travel benefits in the travel business? This book reveals how you can do both without using a dime of your own money. This book shows you how to:

• Start your travel business out of your home in your spare time
• Add a minimum of 50% to your present income
• Travel free, a guest of air and cruise lines and tour companies
• Receive a discount on all airline tickets and hotel bills
• Make a fortune with group travel and much, much more

Use this book to start a new profitable business or just to save money on all your travels. Get this complete hard-bound, 209-page, 9½-by-6½-inch guide for only $20.   #1955

How to Write a Good Advertisement

Victor Schwab

The more books on advertising you study, the better you will be at writing ads. One book I especially recommend is *How To Write A Good Advertisement, A Short Course In Copywriting*, by Victor O. Schwab, one of the best copywriters of this century. He created many famous ads—one, for *How To Win Friends And Influence People*, sold 5 million copies for author Dale Carnegie.

Schwab's techniques are continuously studied by the top advertising agencies, and you should study them, too. Instead of focusing on the structure of the successful ad, Schwab concentrates on the psychology of the consumer. If you know what consumers want and need, your ads will do very well. After reading this book, you should be able to pinpoint the precise needs of your customers and know how to fulfill them. This 227-page, 8½-by-11-inch detailed book can be yours for only $16. #1455

Mike Gilford

The $200 Phone Calls

Mike Gilford

Could you use $200 an hour for just answering your phone? It can be yours for just picking up the receiver and having a four minute conversation. Sit by the phone and wait for calls to come in. This is the most revolutionary money-making system you have ever seen or heard of before. It is a business that allows you to take a 20 percent commission off work you never perform. The people that perform the work are more than willing to give you 20 percent because you will be offering them more jobs than they will ever have time to do. This is a service that is badly needed.

After you receive this book, you too can sit by the TV earning a 20 percent commission while others are out there doing the work for you. #4933 $10

999 Little-Known Business That Can Make You a Fortune

William Carruthers

This book is a collection of 999 businesses that have made their owners rich. It shows you how hundreds of your ordinary talents can be converted into cash and your own business. The majority of ideas require little or no capital and can be started in your spare time. It gives you such a large variety of projects to undertake that you are sure to find that perfect moneymaker for you. Each plan has been carefully selected as a little-known, unfamiliar business that is completely overlooked in most areas of this country. Each is free of competition and has a personality all its own. Use this book to create that special business that will make you financially independent. This book is 5-by-8-inches and has 258 pages. #2155 $10

$200,000 in 24 Hours & 130 Other Moneymaking Reports

Did you ever wonder what companies give you when they offer to make you an instant millionaire overnight? When they offer you instant credit regardless of your past? Well, now for the first time, almost every moneymaking plan and idea on the market has been compiled into one package with reproduction rights, so you can reproduce all or some of these reports. Here are some of the reports you will receive:

- Raise $200,000 in 24 hours without collateral
- Turn bad credit ratings into AAA-1 credit ratings
- Win oil & gas leases in gov't held public drawings
- Profit from a large list of valuable tax loopholes
- Wipe Out all your debts fast without bankruptcy
- Get Rich in mail order, many complete programs
- Stop Paying property taxes! Forever, legally
- Free Subscriptions To More Than 100 Magazines
- Borrow $50,000,000 on your signature for any purpose
- Get Free car, food, clothing, furniture, rent...
- Produce cheap, whiskey, rum, gin, vodka & other liquors
- Convert Your TV into a movie-size screen TV
- Get auto fuel for 15 cents a gallon or produce gasohol
- Purchase a new car for Only $50 above dealer's cost
- Get a $1,000,000 life insurance policy with no cash
- Get an expensive mansion Without Cost
- Get Free Canadian land • Free oil for your car
- Take over a going business with Zero Cash
- Get 300% more on your savings account
- Get gov't land $2.25 an acre • Free Airline Travel
- Strike It Rich with gov't assistance (minerals)
- Own a $1,000,000 corporation in 4 weeks for Only $50
- Buy Gov't Surplus 2 cents on the dollar
- Buy valuable apt., homes & land for next to nothing
- Get All The Credit Cards you will ever want

This is only a small fraction of the reports included. Your kit includes more than 130 full-length reports with reproduction rights. $7 #0333

BUCKLEY BOOKS:
Poor Man's Way To Riches
Volume 1

David Buckley

David Buckley has left a legacy that will enable you to inherit riches. 'Widely regarded as the publisher and author of the best self-help books in the world, he has helped thousands of people rid themselves of former debts and get a fresh start on a successful new life.' The 4-volume set of books entitled the *'Poor Man's Way to Riches'* can offer you this fresh start toward a financially secure future. The first volume of this valuable series contains help on topics that will help you clear off old debts and start on that new financial future. • Have an AAA-1 Credit Everywhere • Borrow Money Fast • Raise Tremendous Amounts of Capital • Make a Million Dollars in Real Estate • Take Over Going Businesses with Zero Cash • Earn $5,000 Monthly by Mail • One-Man Business That Can Make You Rich • How to Avoid Taxes Legally, and more!
#3033 $10.00

BUCKLEY BOOKS:
Poor Man's Way To Riches
Volume 2

David Buckley

Earn $30,000 monthly from oil income • Get a cash loan from your state. • Obtain foundation loans and grants. • Build a $20,000 coin collection from pennies. • Enter a lottery you can't lose. • Get 24 percent on your savings. • Seven offshore big money lenders. • Cash in on Arab money. • Free patents from NASA.
#3133 $10.00

BUCKLEY BOOKS:
Poor Man's Way To Riches
Volume 3

David Buckley

Turn $1,000 into $25,000. • $100,000 in 90 days with discount books. • Invest in machine guns (149 percent a year profits.) • Buy a home for $75,000 and sell for $260,000. • Earn up to $400 an hour from woodcarvings. • Become a new car broker. • $500,000 yearly from cordwood sales. • Sell $2,000 memberships in survival retreats. • Make $50,000 a year with a newsletter digest. • Roll in profits with electric vehicles. • Sell solar energy systems • Make $300,000 yearly with strategic metals.

#3233 $10.00

BUCKLEY BOOKS:
Poor Man's Way To Riches
Volume 4

David Buckley

Make $20,000 a month with debt consolidation. • $1,200 a week with ID cards. • A business making $60,000 a day. • Sell platnium from auto catalytic converters. • Grow big bucks from Jojoba farming. • Make $1,950 daily from photography. • Invest in pennies and confederate money. • Make huge commissions as a patent broker. • $150,000 yearly as a manufacturers representative. • $25,000 part-time from seniors service. • How to make $4,600 in five days.

#3333 $10.00

Pick The Winners

by Paul Lawrence

Can you imagine knowing exactly which horse finishes first before the race starts? This system could put millions of dollars in your pocket every year. It is a 27-part scientific system that is guaranteed to give you results. If you have a calculator and five minutes, you're in business. You could be picking winning horses with this method. Become the racetrack guru with this amazing method. $19.95 #1933

Billion Dollar Modeling Industry

by Jeff Peters

Imagine making thousands of dollars while meeting and working with beautiful women. Women that will beg you to use them in your next shoot. A business where you control the most gorgeous and exotic women in the world. Earn thousands of dollars an hour and you don't even have to do a thing. This book is your ticket to the glamour business of the 80's. It is hot and ready for individuals like yourself to enter. Everything you need to know to make big money in the modeling business is explained to you. #1033 $15

Gray Market Riches

by Dan Webster

Beautiful Porsches as well as Mercedes could be parked in front of your house and could be earning you as much as $20,000 each. Could you ever dream that driving luxury cars could make you so much money? This book will show you how to buy almost any luxury car overseas at a fraction of what it costs in this country. Buy cars overseas without leaving your home. All you have to do is make a simple call to Europe and $20,000 is yours. It is as easy as that. **$39.95** #1733

$15,000 Free For Shopping
by Brad Nolin

Imagine taking home $15,000 each time you go shopping free. That's right, $15,000 for simple shopping that won't cost you a red cent. One man who lives in California became a multi-millionaire overnight, using this exact system. He now takes home $3,000,000 a year. Could you use $15,000 for doing simple shopping? Brad Nolin reveals his incredible method for making this dream a reality. A whole new life of wealth can be awaiting you. #4833 $10

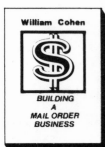

Building A Mail-Order Business

William Cohen

Another highly recommended book is *Building a Mail Order Business. A Complete Manual for Success.* This book covers every aspect of selling by mail, from the basics to the most sophisticated techniques for increasing sales. Every method is explained in a detailed, logical fashion that shows you, step-by-step, how to do it and do it right. This is one of the most complete up-to-date guides on mail-order. Cohen covers product selection, writing, graphics, competition and the legal aspects of mail-order.   #2455 $20

Instant Cash $100,000 Overnight

Jason Hunter

There are millions of dollars awaiting you just for the asking. Banks, the Middle East, and even Africa are desperately looking for people who want money. One of these banks loaned a man with a bad credit history $250,000 to open an Italian restaurant. He now makes $300,000 profit every year. Sources of money you never knew existed will be revealed to you. This is an amazing 260 page, (8½× 11) course that will show you how to get up to $1,000,000 and reveal to you how to get AAA-1 credit even if your credit history is bad. $20

#3433

Money Talks

Jeffery Lant

MONEY TALKS is the complete guide to creating a profitable workshop or seminar in any field. It is written by Dr. Jeffrey Lant, author of a number of important books. MONEY TALKS exposes what it takes to become good at speaking at presentations and how to make money off it. In addition to advice on establishing a business, this book fully explains the profitable products and possibilities such a business offers. The scope of the service (and profit to be made) is truly surprising.
#2833 $30

BEST SELLERS

☐ **$2,000 An Hour**   David Bendah $12.95
(5½ × 8½, 100 pgs.)# 0733

☐ **Cashing In On Government Money** Bill Kerth $10
(5½ × 8½, 100 pgs.)#5003

☑ **Unique Packages**   Pete Branin $10
(5½ × 8½, 121 pgs.)# 1333

☐ **$25 Billion Treasure**   David Bendah $25
(6 × 9, 200 pgs.)# 3633

☑ **Gray Market Riches**   Dan Webster $39.95
1733

☐ **Winning at the Horse Races** Paul Lawerence $19.95
1933

☑ **Seeing Through Anyone**   Tom Foster $10
0533

☑ **Billion Dollar Modeling Industry** Jeff Peters $15
1033

Poor Man's Way To Riches   David Buckley
 ☐ **Volume 1** # 3033 $10
 ☐ **Volume 2** # 3133 $10
 ☐ **Volume 3** # 3233 $10
 ☒ **Volume 4** # 3333 $10

☐ **Money Talks**   Jeffery Lant $30
(11 × 8, 310 pgs.)# 2833

☐ **Tricks Of The Trade**   Jeffery Lant $30
(11 × 8, 316 pgs.)# 5533

☐ **Investment Opportunities For The 1980's** George Sterne &
9403   Russ Von Hoelscher
            $14.95

☐ **How To Achieve Total Sucess** Jeffery Lant $15
(6½ × 9½)# 0933

☐ **The Complete Credit Book** $15
(8 × 11)# 5233

☐ **$15,000 Free For Shopping** Brad Nolin $10
4833

Lion Publishing Company
6150 Mission Gorge Road, Suite 222, San Diego, CA 92120

Please send the above titles. Enclosed is $ _____. If ordering one book, add $1 postage and handling. If you order two or more books, add $2.

Name _____

Address _____

City/State/Zip _____

☑ Selling Information By Mail #3533	David Buckley	$10
☐ How To Use Your Hidden Potential To Get Rich (6 × 9, 200 pgs.) # 0433	David Bendah	$12
☐ Making $500,000 A Year In Mail-Order (Hrd. 6 × 9, 200 pgs.) # 1233	David Bendah	$15
☐ Free Grants And Low-Interest Loans (5½ × 8½), 80 pgs.)#0633	Lloyd Sanders	$10
☑ How to Get Rich In Mail-Order (6 × 9, 116 pgs.) # 2655	Melvin Powers	$20
☐ Building A Mail-Order Business (Hrd. 6½ × 9½, 495 pgs.) # 2455	William Cohen	$20
☐ How To Write A Good Advertisement (8½ × 11, 227 pgs.) # 1455	Victor Schwab	$15
☐ The Self-Publisher's Opportunity Kit (Reprint rights on 8 books & sales material) #1633		$30
☐ 999 Successful Little-Known Businesses, That Can Make You A Fortune (5 × 8, 258 pgs.) # 2155	William Carruthers	$10
☒ $200,000 In 24 Hrs. & 130 Other Money Making Reports (Reproduction rights.) (5½ × 8½, 64 pgs.) # 0333		$7
☐ Make A Fortune & Travel Absolutely Free (Hrd. 6½ × 9½, 210 pgs.) # 1955	Ben & Nancy Dominitz	$20
☐ How To Get Rich In Multi-Level Marketing (6 × 9, 116 pgs.) # 1855	David Holmes & Joel Andrews	$15
☐ Instant Cash $100,000 Overnight (8½ × 11, 260 pgs.) # 3433	Jason Hunter	$20
☐ $10,000 A Month Making PVC Furniture (6 × 9, 80 pgs.) # 2933	Sam Glassman	$7
☐ Home Business Opportunities (Hrd. 6 × 9, 365 pgs.) # 0877	Russ Von Hoelscher	$15
☒ Thousands With Your Camera (5½ × 8½, 88 pgs.) # 2733	Jeff Peters	$12.95
☐ How To Get Anything You Want Absolutely Free Or Next to Nothing (5½ × 8½, 120 pgs.) # 4733	Phil Williams	$10
☐ The $200 Phone Calls (5½ × 8½, 100 pgs.) # 4933	Mike Gilford	$10

Lion Publishing Company
6150 Mission Gorge Road, Suite 222, San Diego, CA 92120

Please send the above titles. Enclosed is $ _____. If ordering one book, add $1 postage and handling. If you order two or more books, add $2.

Name _____

Address _____

City/State/Zip _____